Journey With Jesus

Yong Hui V. McDonald

MAXIMUM SAINTS PRODUCTIONS

Journey With Jesus

Meditations, Reflections, Visions & Dreams

Yong Hui V. McDonald

Journey With Jesus
Copyright ©2006 by Yong Hui V. McDonald
Cover and illustrations by Charles Polk
An inmate at A.C.D.F.

Scripture quotations are taken from
The Holy Bible, New International Version.
Copyright © 1973, 1978, 1984
By International Bible Society
All rights reserved.
No part of this publication may be reproduced,
stored in a retrieval system,
or transmitted in any form or by any means –
electronic, mechanical, photocopying, recording, or otherwise –
without the prior written permission of the publisher
and copyright owners.
First Printing: July 2001
Second Printing: October 2001
Third Printing: December 2003
Fourth Printing: November 2006

Maximum Saints Productions
Website: www.firstlovepress.com
First Love Press: Phone (720) 427-5323
Printed in the United States of America

ISBN-13: 978-0-9790316-0-1
ISBN-10: 0-9790316-0-5

CONTENTS

Dedication
Introduction
Acknowledgements

Part One: Journey With Jesus ...14

Part Two: Journey With Jesus Two...63

Part Three: A Love Letter from Jesus...111

Part Four: A Prayer of Blessing...117

Part Five: The Healing Power of Jesus...118

Part Six: Invitation...122

Part Seven: Beauty of Jesus...130

DEDICATION

This book is dedicated to Jesus, my Lord,
a friend who loves me more
than anyone else I know.
There were times in my life I walked
the road of suffering in grief and sorrow.

When no one else was able to help me,
Jesus offered me a pierced hand
and walked with me.
Jesus gave me what I needed:
peace – peace in my heart,
which I desperately needed while
walking through the fires of life.

This is the story of a person
whom I treasure the most – Jesus.
He gave His life for me so that I can have life
and hope. I gave my life to Jesus.
I even gave my tears so that my stories
can be shared for His glory.

ACKNOWLEDGEMENTS

It's God's grace that *Journey with Jesus* is being published again. The first time this book was published, God provided funding through Korean-Americans. One day I learned that my younger brother was struggling, so I translated *Journey With Jesus* into Korean and sent it to him to encourage him. He was encouraged and inspired by the story, and he shared this story with my mother. Then my mother shared the story with her friends. After reading my story, my mother's friends started giving me mission funds. I believed that God was providing these funds to publish *Journey With Jesus*, so I set aside the money for about a year. Rev. Sandy Blake generously designed a cover for the book, and after that the book was published.

Since then, I have been distributing *Journey with Jesus* to different jails and prisons. That was the beginning of my prison ministry book project. After this book was published, God opened many doors for me to share my faith journey in many different jails and prisons. Moreover, I was able to distribute not only *Journey With Jesus*, but other books I have written as well. I realized the impact of prison book ministry to the incarcerated because they have the time to read and reflect but many times they do not have enough inspirational books.

After I started working as a chaplain at the Adams County Detention Facility (A.C.D.F.) in December 2003, I was more convinced than ever of the desperate need for inspirational books in jails and prisons. A.C.D.F. currently has 1,100 male inmates and 200 female inmates. I receive many requests for Christian inspirational books every day, but we do not have enough books to give them. Our program department at A.C.D.F. is a non-profit organization and chaplains do not have funding for books, so we rely on donations of books.

In our facility, many Christian inmate leaders are leading Bible studies and prayer circles in their pods to help others and want to learn more about the Bible. These leaders request Bible dictionaries, but I don't have enough Bible dictionaries for them. It hurts me when I cannot provide enough inspirational books to help inmates. Because of this shortage of inspirational books, God gave me an idea - I could help the incarcerated by *producing* more books!

I could see God blessing many of the inmates in our facility, and many were experiencing transformation. They were sharing their powerful testimonies, sermons, poems, and prayers in Chaplain's Worship Services, and their stories were touching many people. I encouraged them to write their stories and I gathered them together and made into a book, *Maximum Saints Never Hide in the Dark.* Ten thousand copies of the book were published in February 2006. Many churches and individuals supported this book project with funding. *Maximum Saints* is being distributed in many jails and prisons in Colorado and other States. Not only were our facility inmates and staff inspired by *Maximum Saints*, but also chaplains from different jails and prisons have called and expressed appreciation for the book. A.C.D.F. inmates are greatly encouraged by this book *project*, and they have already started the second book, *Maximum Saints Make No Little Plans*.

The *Maximum Saints* book enlarged my vision for the future prison ministry book projects. Because God told me that my vision was too small when I was going to order 1,500 copies for our facility, I ordered 10,000 copies to distribute to jails and prisons. Because of that, I decided to publish 10,000 copies of *Journey With Jesus* to distribute in jails and prisons.

I am thankful for many churches, especially Park Hill United Methodist Church, supporters of my prison ministry. I thank Ft. Lupton United Methodist Church, Sara Choi, Mr. and Mrs. Desmond McDonald, Son Hui Kim, Hui Chae Lee, Sooja Oh, and many other churches and friends who have given support and funding for this project.

My sincere thanks go to Laura Nokes Lang and Maxine Morarie, Alicia Lewis-Jackson and many other friends who helped me with the editing of this book.

Also, I am grateful to Mr. Charles Polk who drew the cover picture and all the other illustrations for this book. Mr. Polk is an extremely talented artist and has helped many inmates in our facility with his inspirational art work. Many of Mr. Polk's drawings will be in the second *Maximum Saints* book.

I owe my loving husband and my wonderful children for their sacrifice and support for my decision to go into the ministry.

    Most of all, I owe my mother for her great love and prayers. She has been one of the most influential people in my spiritual walk. I believe because of her dedication to God and her persistent prayers for me and my ministry, God has blessed me with many ministry opportunities and with visions and dreams to help the incarcerated with the book project.

INTRODUCTION

When God called me to preach, I told God I would write a book to help others instead of going into the ministry. So, I wrote *Moment By Moment I Choose to Love You*, in January 1998. I thought I was done with God's work when I finished the book, but God did not let me rest. God wanted my complete obedience, but I didn't have an obedient heart. Soon, God was calling me to pray, and I started spending time in prayer. Whenever I went to prayer, I found myself weeping because God kept calling me to the ministry, but I didn't have the heart to follow God's call. This lasted about a year.

During these times of struggle, I started writing *Journey With Jesus*, which was my attempt at understanding how Jesus speaks and walks with me. Some ideas in the story originated from meditations, reflections, visions, and dreams while others grew from an understanding of Jesus. I believe the images, visions, dreams, and understandings originated from God for the following reasons:

First, I am not a creative person who imagines anything different from the ordinary life. Therefore, there was no way I could have written or thought of an allegorical story.

Second, these images and visions in my mind came to my mind after I started spending time in prayer and meditation. I had never experienced this kind of imagery before I made a commitment to spend time with God in prayer.

Third, when the images and visions came to my mind, they always came with deep conviction in my heart, as if God were there and speaking to my heart. I am not saying this to promote and to give credibility to my story, but that God should get all the glory.

Writing *Journey With Jesus* deepened my faith in Jesus. From the start, I was amazed at how much I was able to experience the leading hands of Jesus. I felt so blessed while I was writing the story. I was experiencing Jesus.

Writing my walk with Jesus was a time of reflection and enlightenment for me as I understood how Jesus did take care of me through my struggles and difficult times. The process of writing the story helped me to evaluate my commitment to God. Eventually, it helped me to make the decision to start the ordination process and to pursue my seminary education at The Iliff School of Theology in order to serve God better in the future.

That was ironic because my intention in writing the story had been to understand how Jesus had walked with me. But somehow, the story led me in a direction in which I never had intended to go.

I shared *Journey With Jesus* with others according to God's leading. As time passed, I felt God asking me to share the story with as many as possible. I ignored this request for a while, and when God spoke to me again about this, I asked God, "Why?" I didn't have any desire to make it into a book because the story was personal.

"That story is not yours to keep," God spoke to

my heart. "I gave you that story so you could share it with others. It is the story of how I pulled you out of a pit."

"What pit are you talking about, Lord?" I asked with surprise.

God gave me an image in my mind. At the bottom of a deep, dry well there laid a lifeless little doll. God's big hands pulled the doll out of the well. Holding the doll in the palms of his hands, God breathed life into it. The doll transformed into a little girl, full of life. Then God spoke to my heart, "You were like that doll, lifeless, but I gave you that life."

I understood then that it was Jesus who pulled me out of a pit and gave me life. My heart was filled with gratitude and tears came. I knew no one in the world would care for me as Jesus does.

"You were like that doll, lifeless, but I gave you that life."

Journey With Jesus 13

Part One:
Journey with Jesus

One morning, I arrived at the church around 5:00 A.M. I sang hymns and asked God what I should read, and God gave me Hosea. After I finished reading Hosea, I read some parts of the gospel of Mark, and then I thought it was time to listen to Jesus. I wanted to understand how Jesus had walked with me. This meditation continued many mornings, and it helped me to understand my relationship with Jesus from a new perspective.

I listened to the hymn "How Great Thou Art" and closed my eyes, imagining that I was walking through the woods with Jesus. I didn't expect what I would see next in my mind. I saw a little girl wearing bright, white clothes with no seams, holding Jesus' hand. Jesus was also wearing white robes. The girl looked seven or eight years old and was dancing, jumping, and bounding delightedly. There was tranquility and peace in that green forest. It was a sunny day with a gentle breeze. The girl sang hymns about Jesus, and he looked more pleased than ever. The birds were singing with the girl. Everything seemed perfect in that picture. I knew the girl I was seeing in my mind was me.

That wonderful picture didn't last long. The roads got rougher and rougher. Soon she was walking

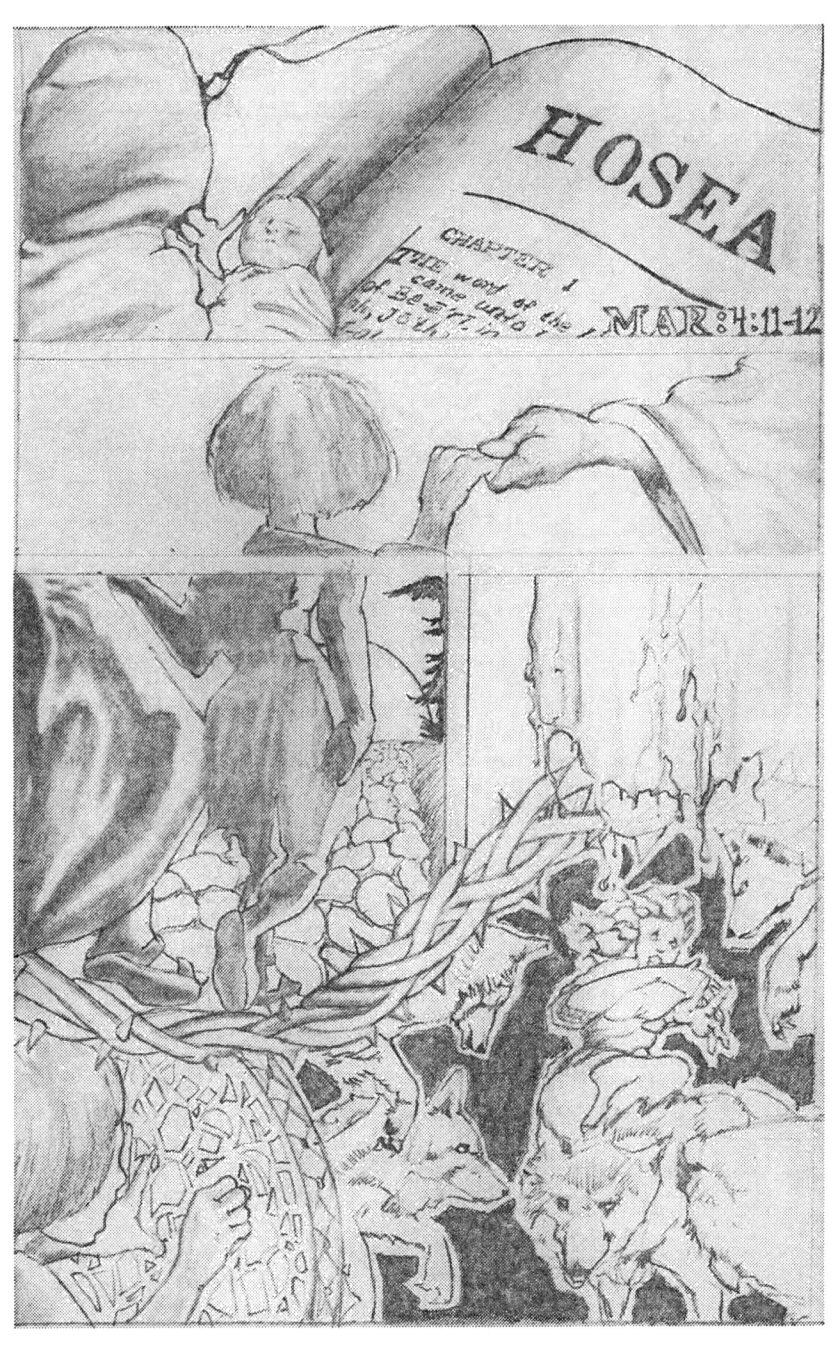

"An unbreakable glass window stood between herself and her mother."

on a road with thorn bushes. Everywhere she turned, there were plants with thorns poking at her. Her dress was dirty and spotted with blood. She didn't understand how she had let go of Jesus' hand. She felt cold, hungry and lonely. It was getting dark. She was frightened by the howls of a pack of wolves. Her heart racing with fear, she walked and walked.

Exhausted, she fell to the ground and drifted into a deep slumber. In her dream, a wolf attacked her mother again and again. An unbreakable glass window stood between herself and her mother. The girl pounded the glass and screamed for help, but no one came. When she finally saw some people in the distance, she desperately called for help. They didn't pay any attention to her, and disappeared quickly from her sight.

"Jesus, where are you? If you are out there please come and help me." Someone woke her up. It was Jesus. She heard his voice calling her name. She felt relieved. He stretched out his gentle, warm hands. He held her hands and led her along the way in the moonlight. When she got too tired to walk, Jesus carried her in his arms until they found a stream.

The sun rose and Jesus gently washed her feet. His eyes were full of compassion, and as he wiped her tears, he also wept. When his tears touched her clothes, her clothes grew clean and no bloodstains were visible. Jesus touched her wounds and her bleeding stopped; she felt no pain. She was convinced that Jesus could heal.

He gave her bread, and she ate. She felt safe

"Jesus carried her in his arms."

Journey With Jesus

and had peace in her heart. He held her hands in his and told her lovingly, "Remember to hold on to my hands always. I love you so much. I want you to walk with me."

"I'm terrified every night. I don't know why my father gets drunk and beats my mother. How I wish I could help her. Can you make my father stop drinking? I know if he quit drinking, he wouldn't hurt my mother," the girl cried.

"He made that decision. I tried to tell your father, but he wouldn't listen," Jesus said.

"I just didn't know what was happening. I thought I would never get out of that place. What was that all about? Did I take the wrong road?" she asked.

Jesus said, "It was the road that you had to follow. Everyone goes through periods of suffering. Sometimes people go through these periods longer than others."

The girl asked, "Jesus, why do people have to walk those roads?"

"Actually, people walk through them because people live in the Fallen World. As you walk along the different roads, there are many obstacles, thorns, and poisonous snakes. Once I lived like you, so I know what you are going through. The best thing about it is that suffering helps people to understand how others are going through suffering. It helps people learn how to help other people."

"Did you have to suffer, too?" the girl asked, noticing nail marks in Jesus' hands. She touched the holes gently with her fingers. The holes felt bigger than they looked.

Jesus answered, "My beloved child, I have suffered and died for you and other people, so even though people suffer in this life, they don't have to suffer in the next life. Walk close to me and hold on to my hand, then I will help you get to our eternal home safely."

Jesus took her hand and started down the road, the road covered with thorn bushes and thistles. Once more she dreamed about her mother being attacked by a wolf again and again. She felt as if she were living in two different worlds, walking with Jesus during the day, but in her dreams, she was alone, horrified.

One day, as they walked along, a group of girls came out and danced, holding flowers in their hands. The girl looked at Jesus and said, "Look at those girls. They have beautiful flowers. I want to have some. I don't know where to get any."

Jesus replied gently, "Those girls have them because their parents gave them the flowers. Their parents are able to provide them love, security, and necessary things."

The girl became sad. "I wish I could have the flowers like they do," the girl said. "Why, Jesus, it seems they all have some, but I don't. You heard one of the other girls teasing me that I wear crummy clothes."

"Child, I know you don't have what they have. No one gave you those, but I will give you flowers when we arrive at a flower garden."

She looked at Jesus' face, encouraged. "Really?

You will give me the flowers?"

"Yes. We have to get to the place where you can pick the ones that you like. Remember, the flowers you will receive in this life are temporary, but the ones I will give you when we get to our father's home are permanent and more beautiful."

The girl felt better. She smiled and skipped with joy as she walked along. She couldn't help but see the other girls' flowers again. How she wished she could have them. She met some friendly girls who asked her to play with them. She was delighted and quickly let go of Jesus' hand. She ran to play with them. As she danced with the others, the girl asked, "Do you know who Jesus is?" They answered, "We don't know who Jesus is." The girl couldn't understand why all those girls didn't know Jesus.

As they were playing on the playground, one of the girls teased her, "You don't have what we have. You cannot be like us. You don't even have any flowers." Humiliated, the girl ran to hide from them. She sobbed as she walked along the road. When she could see no one, she cried loud and long.

The girl knew what she had to do. She was determined to find some flowers for herself. As she wandered around in the forest, she was glad to see wild flowers. When she stretched out her hands to pick them, a snake came out from behind the bush and bit her little finger. She felt sharp pain. Screaming in terror, she raced to get away from that place. She kept running into the thorn bushes, but she didn't care. Her hands and arms became stiff. It

Journey With Jesus

"You don't have what we have. You cannot be like us."

was as if she were dying; she felt danger all over. She knew something bad had happened as she was walking through the valley of the shadow of death. Something had gone totally wrong. She learned that her younger sister who became lost and wandered around the thorn bushes was attacked by the pack of wolves. The wolves crushed her sister on the ground, and she died alone.

Overwhelmed with sorrow, the girl cried and cried for her beloved sister. As the poison spread through her body, she lost consciousness. In her dream, she mourned and dreamed about her sister. Snakes attacked her in her dream. Something was choking her and she struggled to wake up, but she just couldn't. She cried, "Jesus, help me. I need help."

When she woke up, Jesus, with love in his eyes, was holding her in his arms. She felt safe and loved. He gently touched her little forehead and said, "My child, I told you I will get you flowers. Be careful about where you walk and whom you are with. I will take care of you. You should hold my hand always as you walk along. Don't let go of my hand." They sat on the green grass and felt the breeze. The beautiful mountains were reflected on the streams of clear water.

The girl smiled in gratitude. She said, "Snakes were attacking me. They were biting me."

Jesus replied, "I know. Those are not just snakes. They are evil spirits who try to hurt you and other people."

"What are evil spirits?" she asked in surprise.

"There are spiritual realms that you need to know about."

"My child, there's a spiritual world that you cannot see with your own eyes. You can feel it though. When you felt their attack, they really were attacking you. There are spiritual realms that you need to know about. In your journey, you will encounter those evil spirits many times. You can overcome those forces only in my name. If you always walk with me, you will be able to learn how to fight."

"I will stay with you. I don't want the snakes to bite me again. You are the only one who seems to care for me. You are the only one who seems to know how to help me. For a while, I didn't think there was any reason to live. You gave me hope to live. Would you tell me about your nail marks again? I still don't understand why you had to suffer for me."

Jesus looked at his nail marks and looked into her eyes and said, "These are marks that I suffered for you. I died for you so you can be forgiven, so you can have eternal life and live with me in my father's house forever."

Jesus' words had power, more power than anything in the world. For the first time, she saw her true self. Wearing dirty, filthy rags, she felt ashamed of her clothes. Then she realized what Jesus said was true. She was a sinner and needed God's forgiveness. Understanding why Jesus died for her sins, she felt remorse and asked God for forgiveness.

"I died for you, you are forgiven. Now I am alive!" Jesus replied. Then a drop of blood fell from Jesus' nail mark and touched the girl's dress. At once, her ragged clothes changed to a beautiful, glowing

"I died for you, you are forgiven. Now I am alive!"

Journey With Jesus

dress, whiter than snow, and seamless. Her eyes opened wide. She understood how much Jesus loved her. No one would die for her sins. Jesus was the one who not only cleaned her dress and made her feel clean, but he also cleaned her soul. She felt free, as though all of her problems went away. She didn't have any more pain, but instead had joy and peace in her heart. She thanked Jesus again and again for his redemptive work on the Cross.

"Remember your clothes were dirty, but I cleaned them. I washed your sins with my tears and my blood which I shed on the Cross. Now I am alive forever, and I am going to help you to get to our Father's home safely," Jesus said gently.

"What about my sister?" the girl looked up to Jesus. "She walked in the thorn bushes many times and got hurt. How I wished I could give her the flowers to make her happy, but I didn't have any to give her. I saw tears in her big eyes many times when our mother got hurt. I wanted to see her smiling face some day, but now she is dead, and there was no way I can help her."

"She is not dead but alive. She is also one of my children. She is already in our eternal home safely. She is waiting for you, praying for your safe journey."

The girl was comforted, knowing she had something to look forward to. They started walking again. The road was getting worse. As she was passing through a village, some kids on the road gave her a beautiful rose. She was so happy to have a flower. As soon as she held the rose in her hands, the thorns poked her hands and made them bleed.

Jesus looked at her sadly, "My child, throw away that rose because it has thorns. It makes your hand bleed."

"Jesus, that's the only flower I have. I would like to keep it."

"I will provide you with many flowers with no thorns."

"Where would those be?" the girl asked impatiently.

"When we get to a flower garden, you can pick what you want," Jesus smiled.

"I want to keep this one until I get to the flower garden."

"Child, you are hurting and bleeding when you hold on to it."

"I don't understand why my hands bleed. I am not holding it too tight," the girl said.

"It's because, if you hold on to some things, they will only hurt you and make your life worse. Forgetting and forgiving is better than holding on."

The girl then understood. She was holding resentments and an unforgiving heart against those who hurt her. She reluctantly let go of the flower. Then she felt a big, heavy burden on her back lifted. She felt freer than ever. As she started walking with Jesus, she asked, "Lord, why is this journey so long and painful?"

"My loving child, that's what life is about. Look at my hands. I have suffered for you, so you don't have to suffer after this life. You will suffer in this life whenever you go through the valley of the shadow of death. Many people go through the deep, dark valley, and I want you to remember I am always with you. You may not even feel that I am with you when you are sleeping with tears and sorrow. Remember, those are the times that I cry because you are hurting. Hold on to me. I will help you to see that my grace is sufficient in all circumstances. I will wipe away your tears and will give you peace and joy. Just keep walking with me."

"What does suffering do?" the girl asked.

"The times you suffer are the jewels of your crown when you arrive in your eternal home. You will be rewarded when you get to our eternal home," Jesus replied.

"I would like to get to our home fast," the girl said eagerly.

"You have many roads that you have to travel to get to the eternal home, some good and some bad. Keep hanging on to me; then you will be able to handle the situations. You could even be able to help other hurting people along the road."

"I didn't know others were hurting," she replied. "I thought I was the only one who had problems."

"Yes, there are many who need help. I died to save them, and they need to hear the message. Whoever believes in me will be forgiven and receive eternal life. People who don't believe in me will suffer in this life and will also suffer terribly in their next life. That's why I came and died, so they could believe and be saved."

Now she understood what Jesus was saying. The girl knew it was Jesus who had helped her in her toughest times, and there was no question that Jesus died for her to save her from eternal suffering. They came to the desert and the sun was high. It was extremely hot, but somehow she was not bothered by it. Jesus was with her, and he told her many things about himself. She was delighted to learn about him. She knew Jesus meant a lot to her. Occasionally, Jesus gave her food and water. He found a shelter for her when it got too hot. She felt loved. Walking with Jesus was much easier than walking by herself.

Then Jesus talked about how others walking through the desert were not getting any help because they didn't know Jesus. He said, "If you want to help other hungry and thirsty people on the road, I will give you bread and water so you can share with others." Jesus then showed her how much some people were suffering from the evil spirits' attacks. These too she could help with Jesus' power. "You can help them with prayers, and I will help you overcome all these," he told her.

The girl quickly asked, "What about my flowers?"

"If you decide to help these people, it will take longer to get the flowers. I assure you that if you don't get the flowers in this life because you decide to help others, you will receive a hundred times more flowers in the next life in my kingdom."

She thought for a moment. Then she said,

"There are many who need help and they need to hear the message."

Journey With Jesus

"I want to have flowers as soon as possible. I know if I don't have them soon, others will tease me again. I don't want to get hurt any more."

Jesus seemed to understand how she felt. It was a long, rough journey. Jesus taught her more about himself, and he led her to a town called Wonderful Garden City. Jesus answered her prayers. When she saw a beautiful garden, she was overjoyed. She picked many flowers, and Jesus brought her as many as she could hold. She was dancing as she left the flower garden. If she had known she would get all the flowers she wanted, she probably wouldn't have cried bitterly when others teased her. She didn't know at that time Jesus would eventually keep his word. She thanked Jesus again and again. She knew there would be no one else like Jesus. Jesus made a crown with flowers and put it on her head. She felt like she was a princess. Jesus gave her what her parents had denied her.

Jesus gave her bread and juice, and she enjoyed it immensely. Jesus took care of her as he taught her about himself. She became a young woman, and she was about to get married. Somehow she was always a little girl to Jesus, and she didn't quite understand it. As her body and soul were fed, she was satisfied.

She felt loved because her husband loved and cared for her more than anyone else she had met on the road, besides Jesus. There would be no one else like Jesus. Jesus was the only one who could satisfy her soul. Her husband, who loved Jesus, was obedient to him when Jesus told him about the importance of helping hurting people on the road.

Even though Jesus was important to her, she felt resentful when Jesus convinced her husband to feed the hungry. When she tried to change her husband's mind, Jesus told her that her husband was going to fight the good fight, and she should support her husband. So even though it was difficult, she tried to listen to Jesus. Still, she struggled because she didn't care about others who were starving on the road. It would have been easier if she hadn't been there to see when her husband was helping them.

She was thankful that her husband was a wonderful father. Their two children were gifts from God. It was delightful for her to watch how her husband provided love and security to his family. Her wounds were healed as she watched how her husband loved and cared for their children. Her father hadn't been able to give her love and security, but her husband was able to give both to their children. She knew it was all because of Jesus that she received many blessings in life, so she thanked Jesus many times.

Her family life was stable, and she didn't think she needed anything. Slowly, she began to forget about the terrible roads she had traveled and about how Jesus had helped her. Everything seemed to be going well as her family had a picnic every day on the road.

When they approached a town, she saw many nice houses. Up to that point, she hadn't had any desire to have a house or build one. Now her interests had changed. She was heading toward the eternal home with Jesus, but she was getting tired on the long journey. People seemed to enjoy settling down and having homes, so she thought she had every right to enjoy life on earth, just like others.

Wanting her husband to help her build a home, she tried to change his mind about following Jesus' plan, but she couldn't. Even though her husband was doing a good thing, sometimes she was impatient that her husband was busy feeding others instead of helping her. She even told her husband that he should work for something he could see, not for the things he couldn't see. The physical world was more important than the spiritual world to her. Her husband didn't agree with her, though. Before she got married, she asked Jesus for a man who loved Jesus, but now she realized her husband loved Jesus more than she wanted.

Again, without even asking Jesus what he thought about her plan, she let go of his hand. She was determined to build a home without Jesus. As the beams went up and the house began to have a structure, she was thrilled at the thought of living in her own home. She didn't even miss Jesus.

She built a beautiful house, which she loved. Then she started building more houses to sell to secure her future. One day, a tornado came and destroyed all of it. She was shocked. Thinking that she should start a secure building, she learned how to build a house from professionals and started building again. This time, an unexpected flood went through town and destroyed her house. Everything was covered with mud; she felt hopeless. She didn't have flood insurance to cover the loss. Others didn't seem to have any problems building a nice house. Why was she having a disastrous time? She had to pay the workers but didn't have enough money. She cried through many sleepless nights.

Then she remembered Jesus. She had not had any problems like that when she was walking with Jesus. The problems started when she started building her permanent home in that town. She cried, "Jesus, where are you?" Jesus didn't answer, not like other times. She felt she was far away from him. She was desperate. She cried again, "Jesus, come and save me. I need your help. Where are you?" Again, to her disappointment, Jesus didn't come to her.

This time she wondered if Jesus were real. Doubts arose as she desperately looked for Jesus. "Jesus, if you are real, show yourself to me. Why don't you answer me?" she cried. She knew Jesus was real because she had walked with him before. Then a thought came to her mind: if she were to go back and find out where she had lost him, she might be able to find him.

As she was going back to the roads she had come from, she asked different people on the road if they had seen Jesus, but they couldn't help her. Finally, she came to a familiar road; she saw Jesus. He was delighted to see her.

"I am sorry, Jesus," she said. "I didn't know how I lost you, but now I know. I left you here alone.

Now I know you didn't leave me, but I left you! I shouldn't have just relied on my memory of the Scriptures. I thought I knew enough, but I didn't. Now I know I should walk with you and learn about you moment by moment." Jesus had to be the most important person in her life. He was the only one who could satisfy her.

"I have been waiting for you to come back to me. I was praying for you all the time so you could find a way back to me," Jesus replied. "Here, I will wash your feet." She felt Jesus' familiar, gentle hands. Somehow, Jesus seemed to find water whenever he wanted. After he washed her feet, he wiped dry her tears and embraced her tightly. Her body and soul felt clean, and she felt loved.

Jesus looked at her eyes with a smile. "My loving daughter, now remember, we are on a journey to our eternal home, but before we reach there, we have some work to do as we go along."

"What kind of work?" she asked.

"You remember I told you that there are many people who are hungry and thirsty? Many people need to hear that I have died for their sins, so they can believe in me and will be able to live in my father's house with me eternally."

"Lord, my husband is already working for you. Don't you think one out of four is good enough? My two kids are too little, and I have to build a house since my husband doesn't have time to help me."

"If you do my work, I will take care of you."

"Can you wait for a while, so I can finish my

"There will be others who need help along the road."

Journey With Jesus

house that I started building?"

"My child, if you spend all your time building a house in this temporary world, you won't have any time to do more important things, like build your house in heaven. When you work for me and are fruitful, you will be building your house in an eternal home. What's more important? There are many who need to understand my love, and to be saved. There is plenty of work but the workers are few. You sometimes wonder why there is not much good happening in this country? You asked me many times why you don't see miracles in the United States. You asked me why church people's spirituality seems so shallow. That's because people are not willing to work for me, just like you. Many of my children are only interested in their own things, and don't seek the kingdom of God first."

She thought for a moment. Even though she realized that Jesus had taken care of her when she needed help, she now realized that she didn't have much trust in Jesus. She found delight in things that she could see more than the things she couldn't see. She was more interested in material wealth, and she was delighted whenever she could see the improvement on her building.

Knowing that she was not ready to do his work, Jesus suggested that she should spend ten percent of time in prayer every day.

In her prayer time, Jesus taught her about the Holy Spirit who could help her to do Jesus' work. There was no way she could have kept her prayer journey if the Holy Spirit hadn't awakened her in the morning with the hymns, and hadn't kept reminding her to go back to pray when she was getting tired of going to church.

"In her prayer time, Jesus taught her about the Holy Spirit."

Jesus took her by her hand and led her to a remote field where many wounded people were lying and crying in pain. There were nurses and doctors, but there were too many wounded people who were not receiving any care. She was horrified. "You can heal those people as you have healed me. I know you can," she pleaded.

"I have given my power to my workers. The harvest field is ready but workers are few. I need more workers to heal and help these people. This is not a permanent place for you. You don't realize that the house you are building has a shaky foundation. It will crumble when you think everything is fine. There will be others who need help along the road. I want to hire you to do my work, and I will take care of you."

"There were too many wounded people who were not receiving any care."

Journey With Jesus

"Jesus, I cannot do this kind of work. You asked me to pray for them. I will pray for them. I will pray to God so he can send more workers."

"My loving Child, you are expecting your sisters and brothers to fight in the front against evil forces. Think about how many are battling in the war zone. These wounded people are just a few you are seeing. You need to go out to the front to fight the spiritual battle. When you try to avoid your responsibility, you cannot grow spiritually. When you don't fight the battle, there is more chance you could be working for the enemies, because it is easy to be deceived by the devil. You have to put on the full armor of God and fight the good fight. People who put on the full armor of God and fight with my mighty power are the only ones who can win the battle and help other wounded saints. Otherwise, you end up getting hurt like what happened before. You have to learn how to defend yourself when enemies attack you. Many of my children don't know about this battle, and they get hurt. They don't know how to fight and help others. The more you help other wounded people, the stronger you will grow. I will give you more strength when you are fighting against strong enemies. I know you cannot do it with your own power but when you work for me, I will give you power to do it."

"What is that power?" she asked.

"My power is my words. My word is medicine for the wounded people. You are not going out there alone. I am sending you with the Holy Spirit who lives in you. He is the one who will actually change people's hearts and save them. The Spirit frees people from sin and Satan. You have to do the work of spreading the word, so the Spirit can heal people."

She had heard about the Holy Spirit, but until now she didn't quite understand how the Spirit helped people. "Oh, I didn't know that. I thought when I worked for you I had to use my own wisdom and my own strength to do it."

"Nothing you do for my kingdom is done by your power. What I need from you is a willing heart to help wounded people. I have done my work. I died for them so they can be forgiven. All you have to do is to be my messenger to tell others what I have done for them. If you walk close to me and learn from me, then I will teach you how to help others."

"Lord, Jesus, I understand now why you are calling me again and again to do your work. Is it possible that I could make lots of money and help others who work for you?"

"I am the one who provides for all my workers. You don't have to worry about that. I want you to follow me. Now you have to make a choice. You cannot have anything between you and me. You have to choose either money or me. You cannot love both. If you love me, you will feed my sheep."

She knew there was no way she could choose money. Jesus was the most important and powerful person in the whole world. She said, "Jesus, I am sorry. I was very selfish. I was only thinking about myself all those years. I choose you. I am going to work for you. You died for me so my life is yours."

"Now you understand. Remember you will receive rewards in God's heavenly home when you are faithful."

She asked, "What should I do to help others?"

"First, you have to get yourself ready by going through training. You need to put on the full armor of God, and you have to depend on God's mighty power to do the work. The Holy Spirit will lead you and teach you what you have to do step by step. Just follow the instructions. You will be trained every day. You are working for me, first, you need to spend time at least five hours every day with me, so you can learn about me. Read the gospels over and over in order to understand what I have done to save you. You have to listen to me and talk to me in prayer every day. I like to hear your sweet voice. Nothing pleases me more than when my children recognize me by coming to my presence. If my words live in you, I will do whatever you ask. I will show you what you can do when you depend on me."

"Jesus, are you going somewhere? Are you going to be with me while I am working here?"

"I am not going anywhere. I will be with you always. Now you will have to stay close to me all the time to keep from wandering around and getting hurt. Whenever you need me, I will be right beside you. Whenever you need help, just ask me to help you. Remember, you will have to keep walking with me and talking to me by praying. Keep studying my words and they will help you learn about me. Then you will know how to overcome the evil one. My word is like the sword which can help you win the battle. If you don't walk with me, my power cannot work through you. Remember, you have to love me with all your heart, mind, soul, and strength. Don't let anything come between you and me, not even yourself. You cannot follow me if you love yourself more than me. I love you so much, and I want you to love me."

She was walking with Jesus; then she felt heavy loads of burden in her heart. She remembered how her dress had been dirty and spotted with blood in the old days. "Lord, I don't think I can help these people," she cried. "I know I am a sinner. You know I have made many mistakes."

Jesus gently touched her forehead. "My child, all your sins are forgiven. When I died on the cross, all your sins were nailed to the cross and your sins died. When I rose from the dead, your spirit also rose, blameless, clothed with righteousness and holiness. I don't remember your sins any more. I forgave you for my own sake because I love you, and that's why I sacrificed myself for you."

She cried again, "I don't feel like I am forgiven."

Jesus spread his hands, and drops of blood from the nail wounds fell to her dress. Her dress got brighter and brighter, and she felt clean. It was like magic. Deep in her heart, she understood she was forgiven. All of her burdens were lifted from her. She knew then what Jesus said was right. The words of God had power to make her spirit, soul, and body clean. "Thank you Jesus, for dying for my sins. Your words have so much power," she exclaimed with joy.

"Now, you know why I am asking you to go out and tell others about me. Many carry big burdens like you used to. My words have power to set them free from their sins and from the devil. The devil has been lying to people, accusing them, and has many people in chains. Nothing but my words and the Holy Spirit can save them from the devil. Go and tell others that they don't have to carry their burdens anymore. Tell them I died for their sins, and they are forgiven."

They were walking together. Soon, she started weeping, "I just don't think I can do it. I think others might tease me if I say I want to try to help other wounded people. I feel so inadequate. I am only a child. I live in a foreign land. Now I have forgotten my own mother tongue, and I am not good with my second language. Jesus, there are many who could speak so well. Are you sure you picked the right person to do your work? How can I teach others? I am only a child."

"I want you to read the story of Moses until you are convinced that I will teach you what to say, and will give you the words to speak."

After reading the story of Moses over and over, she was convinced Jesus would help her. It wouldn't be her power but Jesus' power. "Yes, Jesus, you saved me many times. You are the most loving and powerful person I know. You saved me from my sins and Satan. Now I believe you can help me to do your work. My life is yours. Use me for your kingdom as you want."

*"Depend on me. Then I will show you wonders,
and I will go out and touch people's hearts."*

She felt so small as she was walking down the road, because she saw many wounded people. She cried, "Jesus, I feel too inadequate to work for you. I don't think I am good enough to do your work."

"My child, that's why I'm calling you to do my work. If you feel adequate then you won't depend on my power, or me, but on yourself. I can only use people who will depend on me, not on their own wisdom, knowledge or abilities. I could even use a donkey to speak. You should rely on me. I will teach you what to speak because I will be with you always. When you feel like you could do it yourself, when you think you could help me with your ability, then realize that you are failing, because you cannot do anything unless my power works through you. My power won't work in people who depend on themselves to do my work. In every step and every situation, depend on me. Then I will show you wonders, and I will go out and touch people's hearts. Just love me and walk close to me. Let's go and help others. Many people are suffering. Help them so they can help others. I called many of my children to work, but they didn't believe my power. Because of their inadequate feelings, many turned away from me. I don't want you to do that. Follow me."

She followed him. It was a sweet communion. Spending time with Jesus gave her such delight; she wondered why she hadn't followed Jesus before. Jesus took her to a huge church where many of Jesus' workers were having a feast. Many sat before Jesus and shared the meal with him. While they were

"Jesus took her to a huge church where many of Jesus' workers were having a feast."

Journey With Jesus

eating, they received instructions on how to help others from the Holy Spirit. When they left, some carried big and others carried small loaves of bread and buckets of water to feed the hungry and thirsty.

She asked, "My Lord, Jesus, why do some carry out lots of food and others carry just a little?"

"My loving child, that's what I wanted to show you. My father has a big bakery in the universe and a bottomless living well. People who carry out lots of bread and water are the ones who listen to my teaching and the Holy Spirit's instruction, and they know how many people they have to feed. They also listen to my words and obey. They live godly lives, and they have more time to feed more people. Those who carry out a small amount of food are the ones who don't spend much time with me. They are so busy listening to the world and themselves, they don't have time to talk to me. So they don't give me any time to talk to them. Consequently, they don't have much time to listen to the Holy Spirit's instruction, and they don't know whom to feed. Not only do they not have time to eat at my table, but they take out only little amounts of food. Their sheep are hungry and thirsty, just like their leader. Follow me, I have something else to show you."

Jesus took her to the outside of the church, and she saw many little bakeries built by different people. Jesus said, "I have called these people to work, but they have their own ideas of how to feed people. Instead of relying on my power and spending time with me, these people started their own bakeries and dug their own wells. What they don't realize is that my bread and water is the only food that can nourish and make people grow spiritually. They don't rely on me. They don't pay attention to my words, and they don't listen to me by praying. How I wish they would talk to me. They listen to the world more than to me. When they are occupied with things other than me, I cannot talk to them. They spend lots of time agonizing about baking bread and trying to draw water from the dry ground, and their flocks are starving. What I want most from my disciples is that they walk closely with me. I want their love more than their devotion to their work. They can bear much fruit if they listen and learn from me. They cannot bear much fruit when they don't walk with me. Many of my workers are hungry and dying because they don't come to my feast. They don't realize that they can only feed others after they have their souls fed by eating at my table. I want you to know this, so you will remember to walk with me; this way you can be fruitful."

She was glad to hear that Jesus wanted to have her always walk with him. She knew how much she was enjoying walking with him. She started singing how much she loved him, and Jesus looked more pleased than ever. She had everything she needed. She had Jesus.

Jesus said to her, "You are my witness. Come and eat at my table."

As she was following Jesus, she took one of her precious stones out of her pocket. They had been given to her as gifts from God a while ago, and she played with them and was delighted to look at them whenever she could. Some stones seemed to be polished and were bright as if they were little lights. Unfortunately, the one she took out had scratches and looked cloudy and dim. She was alarmed and tried to rub it to make it shine like it had before, but she couldn't. She started weeping. She asked Jesus, "Can you fix this? I don't know what happened, but one of my children seems to have forgotten about you. How can this be? I am trying hard, but it doesn't seem to help. Please help me and my child."

Jesus stretched out his hands and said, "Child, why don't you give your child to me so I can help your child."

She hesitated. The stone had her child's name on it, and was too precious for her to give to anyone, even to Jesus. She tried to rub it again to make it shine, but she couldn't. "I don't understand what happened to my child. I would even give my life to make this shine again," she cried and cried. She felt hopeless. She sat on the ground and wept as Jesus sadly looked at her. She didn't want to get up but tried to shine the stone with her handkerchief. It didn't seem to work. Now she seemed to forget that she was supposed to follow Jesus.

Jesus asked her, "Am I greater than your problems?"

She thought about it for a while. Jesus was right. He was greater than anyone else she had met. He was more powerful than anyone else she had met. She said, "Yes, you are greater than my problems." She wiped her tears. Jesus asked her the same question whenever she started crying about the stone.

"My child, why don't you give me all the stones? When you go out to a spiritual battlefield, you cannot work effectively if you carry all the stones you have in your pocket. It will slow you down, and you won't be concentrating on what I want you to do."

"Lord, I gave my life to you so you can use me the way you want. Don't you think that's good enough?" she asked.

"I want you to give me everything you have. You have to hand it all over to me so I can help you to be a better worker for my kingdom," Jesus said.

She got up and took the remaining precious stones from her pocket. Some were prettier than others, and some were just plain rocks. Each had names of her family, her relatives, her finances, her future, her ministry work for Jesus, and many others. She had even forgotten the names of some stones because she had picked them up on the road a long time ago. She gathered all of them and gave them to Jesus. He then put all of them in his pocket and said, "I am going to ask my Father to take care of all these stones for you. I will ask him to shine them and keep them safe while you are going out to the battlefield."

She felt free. She had given all of her problems to Jesus. She was comforted that Jesus would take care of them. As she walked along, she collected more stones out of habit, putting them in her pocket. Jesus told her, "Give them to me. I will take care of them. The problems in your life are tests of your faith. You

Journey With Jesus

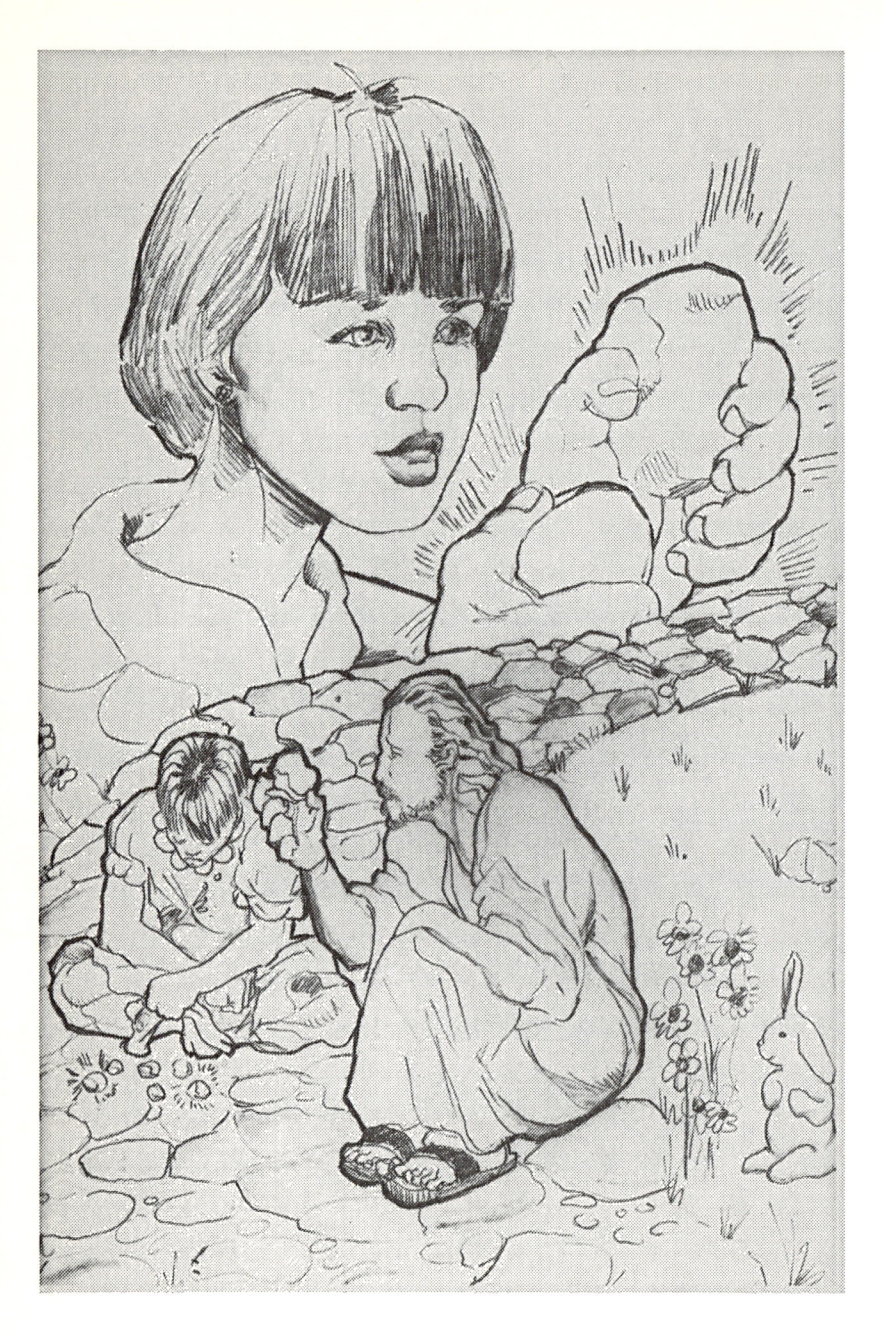

"The problems in your life are tests of your faith."

will pass the tests when you give them to me completely. Don't carry any burdens that you shouldn't carry. I have taken your burdens, and I have overcome the world. You need to take care of others who need help, and you can do it only if you keep giving me the stones that you collect on the way. Come follow me. You are my disciple if you do what I ask you to do."

She sang the hymns of how much Jesus had done for her as she followed him. Her heart was filled with joy when she saw Jesus' smiling face. Soon, they approached a gravel road. She couldn't understand why the nice road suddenly turned rocky. Then the gravel road disappeared; before them were tall, steep mountains covered with rocks and sagebrush.

They started climbing mountains. They had to slow down more than ever because there were so many rocks. She wondered if her journey would ever end. It certainly would be easier if Jesus would move the mountain and make the road straight. She knew Jesus could do that. Jesus had also told her earlier that if she had faith, even she could move the mountains. Where was her faith? She couldn't understand. She expected that everyone would rejoice when she decided to follow Jesus instead of following the world. She was wrong. Her husband, who was also Jesus' disciple and always liked to have her around, was not happy. He said that when she followed Jesus, she might end up working away from him. He was not against her decision, but she knew how reluctant he was to support her decision. How could she make him understand that following Jesus was more important than following her husband's idea?

Jesus knew her thoughts. He told her, "This mountain is called a mountain of testing. Climbing this mountain path is more dangerous and difficult than any other path. I called many people by giving them the desire to serve me and to be my full-time disciples. Many responded. Then, when they arrived here and saw this big mountain, they gave up because they thought they had to move the mountain with their own power. They paid more attention to their environment, listened to their families, listened to other people, and listened to themselves, but they didn't listen to me. Some decided to become part-time workers for their own convenience, therefore, they were not able to do much work. Many wandered around in this mountain for a long time because they were not willing to give up their love for money and worldly desires. In later life, a few realized how they had abandoned their calling and then turned to me and followed me. You will face many fires of testing on this mountain to see if you can be my disciple. Those are purifying fires to help you to be a better disciple. Some turned away from me and abandoned me when they saw the fires. They didn't realize they would only make them strong and mighty in God's sight. Unless you explore and learn about this mountain as you walk with me, you won't be able to move any mountains along the way. Remember, it is I who called you to do my work. Don't let anyone or any circumstances change your mind or stop you from following me. Pay attention to the Spirit's instructions and obey him. Otherwise, you will end up wandering around on this mountain and will grieve me greatly. One of your jobs is to recognize those wandering workers of mine and encourage them to stay on course."

"You are going to teach me how to move the mountains?" she asked.

"Yes, my child. It is I who will help you do that. Pray for your husband and forgive him. I will be helping you to do my work, he will not. I already told you from the beginning that I am the one who will provide all the training and education you need to do my work. The Holy Spirit is your professor and your guide. You shouldn't build resentment against your husband. He is going through the fires of testing which will purify him to make him be a better disciple. To give is to receive. When you forgive, I will answer your prayers. When you pray for him, I will bless him and I will bless you. Test me, and see if I answer your prayers. From now on, I will teach you what is ahead on the road as long as you walk with me. Then, through my power, you will be prepared to move the mountains along the way," he said.

Not long after that, she found a box of colored crayons on the road. She picked it up and on the flat surface of a rock near by started drawing a mountain and trees. A group of travelers passing by stopped and looked at her drawing. "You must be an artist," one man said. She was pleased with the comment; she kept drawing. She thought she must be special and deserve recognition. She was an average art student, but she thought if she practiced more, she could be an artist. She was so involved in drawing that she forgot about Jesus who was standing there, waiting.

Jesus leaned against the edge of the rock and asked her, "Do you remember what I have been warning you about these last two weeks?" The sun was bright, and the gentle breeze moved Jesus' soft hair, his face filled with compassion.

She stopped drawing a house and paused to think what Jesus was talking about. Then she remembered what had happened. As she had spent time with the Lord, she had learned how to take God's bread and water to the hungry. When people started thanking her and showing her appreciation, she became proud. She knew the bread and water were from Jesus, that she was just a carrier. She should have told people to give glory to God; instead, she entertained the thought that she was better than other people.

"Yes Lord, you have been warning me through Peter's and James' letters. I didn't understand why the Holy Spirit kept asking me to read those passages again and again, but now I know. God resists the proud but gives grace to the humble. I didn't realize how others' recognition could bring out my proud attitude. I am very sorry. I don't know how you can put up with me. Please forgive me. I learned that I didn't have a forgiving heart, and now I am learning that I don't have a humble heart."

"Remember this. If you look for praise or

recognition from other people while feeding my sheep, you will be working for yourself, not for me or for my kingdom. In fact, some of my workers love their work more than me. They love praise from people and forget about praise from my Father," Jesus told her. "I have abandoned many of my workers because they served themselves instead of serving me. Some of them don't realize the power of the Holy Spirit and rely on themselves, so they are not effective in their ministry. Some experience the power of the Holy Spirit, become proud and give themselves the glory which belongs to me. So the Holy Spirit abandons their ministry, and they cannot be effective anymore. I give the Holy Spirit to my children so the Spirit can teach them and they can be my witness, not to feed their self-glorification or pride. I give power to my workers to go out and tell others about me, so they can release the Holy Spirit's saving power to free people from sin and Satan."

"A while ago, you helped me to forgive others by helping me to understand other people and situations. Please help me so I can have a humble heart," she said, tears rolling down her cheeks.

"Most of the time, when someone is praised and honored by other people, they are not the one God will praise and honor. Show respect to everyone because you don't know whom God will honor and praise. Also, when you praise people in front of others, it will create jealousy, resentment, and discouragement among my workers. The devil creates division among my people because of that. That's why

I said anyone who wants to be the first must be the servant of all. So be careful what you do to others and to yourself. If you remember to give God glory for all the work you do for my kingdom, then the Holy Spirit will work with you, and you will bear lots of fruit."

"Jesus, I am learning that if I could see myself the way you see me, then there would be no room for boasting or a proud attitude." she said, looking up into Jesus' gentle eyes.

"There is one thing of which you can be proud. You can be proud of me because of what I have done for you. Anything else that makes you proud or boastful will lead you to fall. You cannot even boast about your accomplishment because you wouldn't be able to accomplish anything without the help of the Spirit. As you know, the Spirit is the one who opens peoples' hearts and saves them. You know that you cannot do anything productive for my kingdom without me. Your obedience will be rewarded in my Father's heavenly home. Your best reward on earth is to walk with me, guided by the Holy Spirit, so you can see my mighty power going out to save people. If you receive all the glory and recognition from the people on earth, you don't get any reward when you reach my Father's house. The Holy Spirit's power will work through you when you are willing to obey the Spirit's leading and to do what I asked of you with a humble heart," Jesus said.

Not long after Jesus had this conversation with her, the girl's friend came and asked her to bring some more bread and water to feed the hungry. The girl hesitated. She then remembered what Jesus had told her before. He told her to rely on him at every step and every situation, so she asked, "Jesus, I don't know if I should feed other people anymore. Wouldn't it be better if I just ignore her to save myself from falling into the sin of pride? Do I need to tell others what I learned from you?"

Jesus replied, "Yes, you do need to feed the hungry. That's why I have called you. Tell them what you have learned, that will feed the hungry souls. If you don't tell them, I will raise others up to tell them. There are many people who need to hear what you have learned from me. Some of my children have forgotten me, and you need to remind them that I am the one who feeds the hungry souls through my workers. They need to hear that I am alive and that I care about them."

"My Lord, Jesus. My sins of pride and a boasting heart are not my only problems. I am also afraid of other people's criticism. There will be some people, even Christians, who won't be able to understand me. They will mock me when I share about my walk with you and what I am learning from you," she said.

"My daughter, don't be afraid of others' rejection or criticism. I am always with you. Just tell them that I asked you to share what you have learned from me. You have to listen to me, not to people. You have been asking me why you don't see a big revival in America. There have been revivals in some parts of America, but my desire is to have more of them. I am looking for a tool that can be used by the Holy Spirit to touch many people's hearts, so that they turn their hearts to me and my Father. That tool is someone who will listen to me, not to the people. I want you to keep praying for revival. Your prayers will be answered when I find enough people who will give all their hearts, all their minds, all their souls, and all their strength to me for my kingdom and for revival of this country. You could be a part of that revival if you are willing to give all of yourself and to pay attention to the Holy Spirit's leading. Rely on my wisdom, not upon your wisdom," he said.

That made sense to the girl. She realized she was not indispensable. Jesus could raise anyone to accomplish what he wanted to be done. Jesus loved her, and he was not going to force her to do anything she was not willing to do. She didn't have to be afraid of people because Jesus was with her. She had a choice of being obedient or disobedient. She chose to be obedient. "Thank you, Jesus. You have answered my questions. I will feed these people," she said.

"Come and follow me. I will show you how much work we have to do before the biggest revival begins. I want you to reach out to people no one else reaches out to, because that's where my lost sheep are," Jesus said, stretching out his hands. He held her hands tightly. "My child, I love you. I will be with you and take care of you."

The girl was delighted to hear what Jesus had said. Her heart was filled with admiration for Jesus, and she said, "You are the most important person in my life. No one else in the world loves me as you do. You died for my sins, so that I could be forgiven. You are walking with me, so that you can lead my way to the heavenly home. You are helping me to help others, so they can also find the way to your glorious heavenly home. Jesus, you are the best. Thank you for being with me. I have everything I need because I have you."

She started skipping and dancing while squeezing Jesus' hands. Jesus' face glowed as he started skipping and dancing with her. She looked into Jesus' eyes and started to sing to him, "I praise you and love you, Jesus, with all my heart. I love you more than yesterday. You have power over everything. If you ask me what I want, I want revival in this country. Holy Spirit, open people's hearts so they can understand they are sinners, and repent, and be saved. Jesus, I give you glory, praise, honor, and thanks, because you deserve it. I love you more than yesterday." She knew walking with Jesus was difficult sometimes, but she also realized walking with Jesus was the most wonderful and glorious walk she could have.

"Come and follow me. I want you to reach out to people no one else reaches out to, because that's where my lost sheep are."

Part Two: Journey with Jesus Two

INTRODUCTION

I used to say that if everyone were like me, there would be no pastors. Jesus changed my heart. Still, I had many questions before I started the Iliff School of Theology.

One question was whether God wanted me to attend school at this time. In order to attend Iliff in Denver, Colorado, I had to drive six or seven hours on Monday to attend classes, stay through Thursday, and drive back home that night. Our daughter was fifteen and our son was twelve. Would my husband be able to handle the work and the kids? Would it be better if I waited until our children got older?

While struggling with these questions, different images came to my mind. I believe God gave them to me because those images had spiritual lessons for me. I finished writing Journey With Jesus, but I didn't do anything about it for a while. When those images kept coming to my mind, I thought God was telling me that I was not done with the story; I started writing Journey With Jesus Two.

To my amazement, Jesus answered the questions I had concerning school while I was writing the story. Thus, I was able to go to school with peace of mind, believing that God was directing me to go to school.

Like Journey With Jesus, I felt blessed while I was writing Journey With Jesus Two. As I was writing, I became aware that most of my stories were evaluating my life, mostly my failures. Why? If Christ was leading me and I had more commitment to follow Jesus' calling, should I not see a more successful and comforting journey? Strangely, the answer was negative.

Some of my friends who read my stories told me that Journey With Jesus Two helped their spiritual journey more than the first one because it explained what they should watch out for as Christians. But one friend told me that the first one was positive but the second one was negative, and I agreed with her. She was my good friend, and I valued her opinion so highly that I decided to discard the story.

However, before I put the story away, I reviewed the lessons I learned. That changed my mind, so I decided to keep it. Journey With Jesus Two gave me a new perspective of myself, other Christians, and Jesus. The most important lesson I learned was this: Jesus is willing to work with a person, even a person of failure.

Before I started writing Journey With Jesus Two, I thought I had lived a pretty good life; therefore, I considered myself a pretty good Christian, according to my own standard, of course. While I was writing, I realized I failed miserably as a Christian because I was naive and ignorant about the dangers Christians have to go through.

I understood the spiritual world from my early

Christian experience, and I should have paid more attention to my spiritual walk, but I only paid attention to the physical world. I accepted Christ and experienced his love and forgiveness, but I didn't realize that I had to have a total commitment to follow Jesus. Consequently, when I felt God was calling me to the full- time ministry, I resisted. I wanted to follow my desires and those of the world.

The price of not walking with Jesus was high. I paid the great price for my weaknesses with regret and remorse. I learned that it is good to be reminded of our mistakes, but not to beat ourselves with the sins that we had repented and that had been forgiven. We just need to remind ourselves not to make the same mistakes. In that sense, it was good that Jesus helped me to evaluate my life.

Actually, from the beginning, I was aware that the story of Journey With Jesus Two was an answer to my prayer. Previously, I had asked God to help me to see myself the way He sees me. I learned that God sees me differently than I see myself. I was humbled when I realized that I didn't even recognize my own mistakes until Jesus helped me to see them through the story. Jesus knew all my faults, but he always willingly helped me. He was so kind and gentle when I didn't even deserve it. It was, however, painful to go back and be reminded of my mistakes, but I learned that it was necessary for my spiritual growth.

I learned that the reason Jesus was calling me to do his work was not because I lived up to His expectations, but because His grace is greater than my shortcomings. Jesus accepts and forgives people who fail him, and he even calls them to serve him. I learned that unless Jesus reveals our sins, sometimes we don't even realize how much we are grieving God. That helps me to have more compassion for other Christians who make mistakes and don't even realize what they are doing.

I give God all the glory for what he has done in my life. Without Jesus' love and power, I know I would not have the peace of mind that I have now. Without Jesus' encouragement and assurance, I know I wouldn't have the courage to follow him. Without Jesus' compassion, I know this story couldn't have been written.

Reflections

I was driving to school one morning in Denver and saw a little girl, two or three years old, holding her father's hand, going into a store. The father opened and held the door so the girl could walk in. She was so little and helpless, there was no way she could comprehend her father's feelings and thoughts. Seeing that, I realized how little I would understand my heavenly Father, even when I would try so hard. But the love of the man showed toward the little girl was something I needed to remember. God, my loving Father, was leading my life, and He would care for me as though I were a little child. Realizing that, I broke down in tears. Even if no one cared, I knew God would care for me. I needed that assurance.

The scene of the father and the little girl stayed in my mind for many days and reminded me how much my heavenly Father loves me. It also reminded me of my relationship with Jesus. I was a young woman, but whenever I saw myself with Jesus, I was a little girl, holding Jesus' hand.

For a long time, even after I became a Christian, I was walking by myself. I thought my ideas were better than Jesus'. I wanted to follow my plans, took a wrong path and wandered around the desert in despair. I was headed toward the wide road of destruction, but Jesus called me and turned me around. Since then, I learned why I fell away from the Lord, why I didn't feel the presence of God in my life, and why I had a big empty hole in my heart. It was because I was not walking with Jesus.

I learned that there was no way I could ignore Jesus and be happy because he was part of me. I wouldn't be able to feel whole without Jesus because the empty hole I had in my heart was a place prepared only for Jesus. I knew I desperately needed Jesus to walk with me so I could listen and talk to him.

Jesus knew how to help me better than anyone else I had met on the road. He had taken care of me whenever I had gotten hungry or thirsty. Whenever I had walked on the dirt road, he washed my feet, as he always had. He had forgiven me when I had made mistakes. Jesus' blood had so much power to clean my heart. I knew there was no one else like him. He loved me so much he had even given his life by dying on the cross to take my place so I can be forgiven.

After Jesus finally convinced me of how important it is to feed the spiritually hungry and thirsty, I told him I would serve him. But I didn't realize how much he had to teach me until I made that final commitment to follow him. One thing I knew for sure: Jesus would always be with me, so my journey with Jesus continued.

Journey with Jesus Two

The girl asked, "My Lord, I want you to help me see me the way you see me, so I don't fall away from you again." The air was fresh, and Jesus' face was bright with a gentle smile, his eyes filled with love and compassion.

Jesus said, "My beloved daughter, I will show you how I see you and tell you the dangers for people who decide to follow me. The devil knows whom I have called to the ministry and tries to encourage my workers to abandon their calling. One thing you have to learn is not to love the world, but to love me. I will show you what happens when people love the world. Come, follow me."

Jesus showed her a game room which had a spinning metal rod, surrounded with sharp blades. Many people had tried to hold or touch the blade, and the blade cut through their bodies.

Jesus turned to the girl. "People play this game because they believe gaining money, wealth, and worldly things will lead to security. Many try to obtain worldly possessions to gain security, but the only security they can have is when they have me; I am the only one who has the power to save their souls and give eternal life. When people are satisfied with worldly possessions, they tend to forget about me and my kingdom. Do you realize why I have brought you here?"

The girl cried, "Jesus, I tried to grab a blade, and I got hurt. I was relying on money, and not on you. Please forgive me."

Jesus replied. "I forgive you, my child. In the midst of your backsliding, my grace carried you out of that room. Your financial trouble was a blessing to you. Without it, you wouldn't have started praying to me. You would have kept heading toward destruction. You were about to collapse on the floor, but I snatched you out of that room and healed you."

"I'm so sorry, Jesus. I listened to the world and myself but not to you!"

Jesus said, "When people listen to me by reading the Scriptures and praying, they are leaving that game room and being healed of their wounds. Once saved and healed from their wounds, they can help others get out of that place. When people end up dying in that game room, their spirit will be carried and tortured by demons forever. Many of my followers have turned back to the game rooms when they faced financial trials. They chose worldly comfort over me, bringing spiritual destruction. I cry when they don't understand why they are getting hurt, falling, and being beaten by the devil."

"Jesus, my problem was that I didn't know I was hurting myself because I had to take care of our family's financial needs. My husband didn't make enough money, and you know how much my family suffered because of it."

Jesus asked her, "While your husband was feeding the hungry, was there any time you didn't have enough food for your family?"

"No, Lord, we always had food. That was not our problem."

"My daughter, many of my workers fast when they don't have enough food to eat. And I am telling you they are richer than those who have enough food. In fact, my workers fast and eat according to my wishes. They know their reward is not in this world, but rather in the heavenly home. By experiencing trials and difficulties, my workers will learn my love and get strength through my power. I will always be your comforter and provider. I want your total commitment to me. When you work for me and for my kingdom, I will take care of you."

"My Lord, Jesus, the only way I made money was to work for other people. Are you asking me to work for you only? Some people work different jobs to support themselves."

Jesus said, "There are some I call to work to earn money to serve my people, but I am calling you to tell others about my love. If everyone worked only for temporal things, who would take care of the spiritually sick, the hungry, the wounded, and the dying people? I call my workers to share my love and power with others. I was training you to do my work when I sent you to school. I showed you the spiritual world to motivate you to go out to help the wounded people with my power. You experienced the power of my words. When you were backsliding and followed the wide road, money became your god. Making money was the center of your attention, not me. You didn't think about what I wanted you to do. When you worked for someone else, you had little time to do the things I wanted you to do. What did you accomplish while following the world?"

"Lord, I thought I was accomplishing a lot at that time, but as I look back, I see I didn't accomplish anything. I didn't even realize that I was going the wrong way. Now I am worried about how we can manage our finances. My seminary education will cost so much."

Jesus answered, "Is not everything mine? Why worry so much. I will provide all the money you need for school. I train my workers, and I pay for their expenses. Didn't I pay for all your school expenses before? I promise you that I will take care of you when you follow me. You will learn how to be content because my grace is sufficient for you. When you are willing to suffer and face difficulties for me and my kingdom, you will be spiritually rich in this life and rich in my Father's kingdom."

Jesus was right. There were times she thought it was impossible for her to continue in school, but Jesus opened the doors and provided everything she needed.

"Thank you, Jesus. You have helped me so far, and I am glad that you are going to help me again. Thank you for healing me from backsliding. How can I make sure that I won't deceive myself and go back to that game room again? How can I know when I love something more than you?"

"When you try to follow the Holy Spirit's

directions, you, yourself, circumstances, and other people will try to hinder you. When you are filled with fear and cannot obey the Holy Spirit, that is your blocking stone. That blocking stone is what you love more than me. If you have something and are afraid of losing it, that is what you love more than me. Do not have any fears because I will be with you. From time to time, the Holy Spirit will open others' hearts to let them know that you are walking with me. You don't have to worry about what you will lose because you don't own anything in this world. If you think you do, the devil has already fooled you. The prince of this world will try to make you believe that if you work hard and forget about me and worship worldly things, you will have all the riches in the world. But no one but me owns anything. Even Satan has only as much power as I give him. Anything I give you in this world is for you to use in serving me and my kingdom more effectively. If you love anything more than me, it will become your trap. You cannot even love your life more than me. Loving yourself more than me will cause you to pay more attention to your own desires than to my plans for you. Do you realize that your attitudes and your heart are against me? When I ask you to do something, you try to reason spiritual matters with your own wisdom, and you just cannot understand it. Thus you disobey the Holy Spirit. That's why you have to renew your mind with my words and be instructed by the Holy Spirit. Then you will be able to do what I ask you to do. In order to bear lots of fruit, you shouldn't love the world. You have to die to the world."

"Lord, how can I die when I am still alive?" she asked.

Jesus answered. "To die is to die to your own fear. Then what matters is to do God's will."

"My Lord, Jesus, when I decided to follow you, I thought I only had to give myself, but I am learning that even my family, my relatives, and my friends have to sacrifice part of their hearts and lives. That was not what I expected."

"When I call one of my children to serve me, I also call people around them to sacrifice their lives to serve me. Your commitment to serve me challenges their faith and commitment to my work. The more commitment I demand, the more sacrifices there will be, but many don't want to sacrifice themselves for me or for my kingdom. Without sacrifice there is no gain. My sacrifice brought you out of the kingdom of darkness and into my kingdom of light. It broke the chain of sin and death and released you from Satan so you can walk with me. By giving your life for my kingdom, you will grow spiritually and learn to encourage others to follow me. You have received many spiritual blessings due to my sacrifice on the Cross and the sacrifices of others for my kingdom. That's the sacrifice I am asking of you. You will not only have to sacrifice your life, but you should also encourage others to sacrifice their lives for me and for my kingdom, so my lost sheep will be found. I will take care of you and those around you. They will sacrifice their time with you to serve me from time to time while you take care of the sick, wounded, and those in need."

"Jesus, I thought my tears of offering were good enough when I decided to follow you, but I am learning that my decision to follow you would cause my loved ones to cry. They are being forced to sacrifice part of their lives for me."

"My child, you misunderstood. They are not sacrificing for you but for me and my kingdom. Their tears will become their blessing. You need to understand that without tears, there would be no healing. When you were weeping before me because you didn't want to obey the Holy Spirit's calling, your tears purified your motivation and healed you of your worldly desires. Your tears helped you to be aware of your spiritual condition; the tears you and others shed will bring healing to many people. Whenever you cry, I cry, too. Someone has planted the gospel seed, watered it with tears, and prayed for your healing. I listen and answer my children's tears of offering."

"I didn't realize others' tears bring my healing," the girl said.

Jesus replied, "My tears and suffering brought reconciliation between people and my Father. People who sow in tears will reap with songs of joy. It is time to go out and sow the seed of tears. You need to plant my seeds of love so others can understand how much I love them. You have been asking me to give you a heart of God because you want to hear what I hear, you want to see what I see, and you want to feel how I feel. Think about the people in the game room. How many are crying out for help? Not many have concern for those wounded, hurting, dying, and suffering people. How can you have peace in your mind when the evil spirits torture my beloved people? How can you have joy in your heart when you know many are spiritually naked, wounded, and headed toward eternal torture and imprisonment? How can you sleep when my people refuse to respond to my calling because they love the world more than me? The harvest is plentiful, but the workers are few. See, if you have my heart, you will be weeping all the time. Your tears of compassion are the seeds of love that will bring healing to others. You will see miracles when you sow the seeds with tears. In the midst of weeping, I give peace, joy, and strength to my people. You won't always comprehend how I feel but sometimes I will allow you to understand how I feel, so you will understand who needs you, when, how, and why you should help. Now it is time to go out to look in the bushes to find my lost sheep and heal them."

"Jesus, why do I have to extend myself so much to reach out to people when I have enough work to do around my home and church as a pastor's wife?"

"Many who attend church are already healed. They need continual care, but the ones who need the most help are not in the church. Many of my lost sheep are hungry, thirsty, frightened, hurting, crying, weeping, and wailing in the desert where the scorpions and snakes roam. They need my care. I know where they are, and I see their tears of despair. Many wounded sheep are wandering around in the thorn bushes and the lonely streets where the wolves search for food. Many brokenhearted people cry for help, and I am the only one who can cure them. I need my workers to go out to heal them with my medicine of love and power and to bring them safely into my heavenly home. My medicine is free because I have already paid for it with my tears and blood. The Holy Spirit will lead you so that you can reach out to the people I want you to reach out to."

"Lord, not everyone approves of following you the way I am following you now. It seems it was much easier for my family and my relatives before I made a commitment to serve you. Now there is more struggle."

"Do you remember, I said I didn't come to bring peace but a sword, division, and fire? People who love their father or mother more than me are not worthy of me; people who love their son or daughter more than me are not worthy of me; and people who don't take their cross and follow me are not worthy of me. Whoever finds their life will lose it, and whoever loses their life for my sake will find it. I want your total devotion for me and my kingdom. Without complete surrender to the Holy Spirit, you will wander around in the desert and try to do what you think or what others think you should do. Don't pay any attention to others when they try to discourage you from following me. The Holy Spirit, not others, will help you to do my work. The Holy Spirit will go out and open people's hearts when you obey the instructions. Now you have to make a decision as to whether you will follow me or the world. You will face this question again and again until you consider yourself dead to the world but alive to me. If you look for others' approval, you will end up following the world. Did any of my disciples ask for approval from anyone when I called them to follow me? If they had, I know many wouldn't have followed me."

"Lord, some people try to convince me that I should just help my husband in the church."

"That's because they don't understand why I have called you to the ministry."

"You know it, Lord. Then why don't you tell them that you have called me to the ministry?"

"There is a reason why I don't tell them. It is for their benefit as well as yours. You don't quite understand why I called you to the ministry and how I am going to use you in the future. You have to follow me one step at a time. Through this experience, you will learn to depend on me, not others. Others, who don't understand you at this time, will also learn to depend on me, not their own understanding."

The girl replied, "My Lord, Jesus, help me so I can depend on you."

Jesus smiled. "Don't be afraid of anyone because I am with you. Just follow the Holy Spirit's directions. I am going to say this again: others around you will grow spiritually because of your commitment to serve me. I will show them that I am alive and that I care about them. My fire will purify you and the people around you. Follow me. I have many things to show you."

Jesus led her to a beautiful town. Along the roads all types of flowers and trees were blooming. Colorful birds and wild animals could be seen along the banks of the stream that flowed through the town. People in the park were enjoying the beauty of nature. There were many houses in that town. Jesus stopped and knocked on the doors marked with a cross, but no one would open the door.

Jesus said to her, "My child, many people in this town believe they are good Christians, that's why they display a cross on their doors. But they don't know me or believe that I died to save them. You need to tell them what I have done for them; they need healing."

"Jesus, I thought you wanted me to reach out to the people who are wounded and dying. Those I saw through the window don't seem to suffer from anything, so why should they listen when I tell them that they are sick and need a doctor? They will mock me if I tell them that they need you."

Jesus looked at her with a sad look in his eyes and said, "My daughter, you are only seeing what you can see. They seem to be doing fine outwardly, but deep inside they realize how empty their hearts are. They need to see themselves as I see them: naked, pitiful, and having sores all over their bodies. There are many lost sheep in this town. People who depend on themselves fall into destruction. When people focus on doing only good things and forget about me, they are not walking with me. They need to depend on me and my redemptive work on the Cross, not my hand, you are safe." He assured her.

Jesus was so powerful. His words gave her such peace of mind that she forgot she was walking on the water. In that dark place she saw some lights shining from different sizes of ships shaped like churches. Lifeguards on the ships, who wore glowing garments, threw lifesavers and pulled people out of the river. Some were walking on the water as easily as walking on land, and they were listening to the Holy Spirit's instructions about how they could help people.

"I called those rescuers to serve me, and they willingly went to save dying people. They are the little lights reflecting my light," Jesus said proudly. "I called them to shine their lights so that others can find a way to my Father's heavenly home."

"Jesus, why do some glow more than others?" she asked.

"Those who have brighter shining clothes are living godly lives, obeying my words, and obeying the Holy Spirit's leading. The greater the commitment they have for me and my kingdom, the greater is the light that shines from them. When people have less commitment for me and for my kingdom, less light shines from their life, and only a few come to know me and to be saved."

The girl understood why she was not able to bring many people to Christ. She was not listening to the Holy Spirit's leading and didn't pay much attention to the words of Jesus to reach out to the lost souls. "I am sorry, Jesus. My lack of commitment to your calling caused me to ignore the lost people. Help me so that I will be able to reach out to people as you would want me to."

"My daughter, your obedience to the Holy Spirit's instruction will help you to bear fruits. Come, I need to show you what you have to learn in order to be my disciple."

As they passed more ships, they reached one that looked like a church outside, but inside, it looked like a bar. Under the dim light people were dancing to worldly songs. The music was so loud that they didn't seem to hear others crying for help.

Jesus said, "There are quite a few lifeguards in this ship, but they are not concerned with drowning people. I call many to be rescuers, but only a few respond to the need and undertake the extensive training. In order to be rescuers, people would have to saturate their hearts and minds with the words of my lifesaving manual and learn about my love and power. Unless they understand my love for them and for others and believe my words have the power to save people, they will drop out of the course. Even after they finish the training, they have to hold my lifesaving manual in their hearts so that they can tell others about my love. Many put away my book and start carrying the worldly manual written by people influenced by the devil. They deceive themselves by thinking that human reasoning should be placed higher than my lifesaving book. These lifeguards even bring the devil's teaching to my people in the church and say sinful attitude and behavior is godly. Many stumble and fall because of the fallen leaders of the church. The problem is worse when those fallen lifeguards throw my book of life in the garbage and cannot realize that when they do that, they throw themselves in the garbage can, too. They start living filthy and disgusting sinful lives."

The girl understood why Jesus had brought her there. She said in tears, "Jesus, now I realize that one reason I followed the world and fell into sin was because I didn't hold on to your words. I was listening to the worldly standard, not your words. Please forgive me."

"I forgive you, my daughter. When people don't have my words in their hearts, they don't have the power to live godly lives. My words purify peoples' thoughts, motivations, attitudes, and actions. But I have not given up on these fallen workers. I am still knocking on their doors today, and the Holy Spirit is trying to bring other Christians in their way so they can repent. I pray that they will come to an understanding of what kind of spiritual condition they are in and turn to me. When people don't recognize my word as the most powerful saving book, they start working against me and the Holy Spirit, who is the caretaker of the church."

"Lord, Jesus, how can I know that the Holy Spirit is working in my life? For a long time, I didn't realize that I had to pay close attention to the Holy Spirit's leading."

"My child, the Holy Spirit uses my words to speak to my children in a small voice in their hearts, but many don't understand this and ignore the Holy

Spirit. The Holy Spirit lives in you and can guide and comfort you. People don't obey the Holy Spirit because they follow their own desires, not what I desire for them. Many times what the Holy Spirit asks them to do is contrary to what people want to do."

"Lord, help me to hear clearly the voice of the Holy Spirit, and help me have the courage to do what you are asking of me."

"Unless people start paying attention to my words, they won't be able to hear the Holy Spirit's voice. Remember this: if you look for me earnestly, you will find me. You will be able to hear my voice if you try by reading the Bible and praying diligently. Still, there are other dangers you need to be aware of. Come, I will show you."

They walked toward the other ships, and she heard a loud noise coming from a ship close by. Jesus took her to a ship where a mob of people was chasing a wounded lifeguard. When the people grabbed the lifeguard, they beat him until the man fell to the floor, then they threw him into the river. A few of Jesus' workers, who were walking on the water, pulled the wounded man to another ship to help him. Inside the ship, a mob of people was divided into two groups. In one group were followers of the lifeguard while in the other were people who had gotten rid of the lifeguard. They accused each other and started throwing the church furniture at each other. Some fell into the river, and no one noticed.

The girl was shocked. "Jesus, what happened here?"

Jesus replied, "My daughter, many of my workers are accused, stabbed, chased and beaten by the people in the church. Those who hurt my workers may attend the church, but they belong to Satan. Sometimes even my children are deceived, make wrong judgments, and hurt my workers. I sent my workers to help other Christians rescue drowning people. Too many of my rescuers are discouraged, burned out, and have left the work I have for them. When church people back stab their spiritual leaders, they don't realize they are inviting the devil's attack. They are opening their hearts to the devil, who will help them plant seeds of unforgiveness, resentment, and ungodly manners. Sowing bitter seeds in their hearts will choke my people to spiritual death. Also, the devil encourages people to leave the church by telling them that there is no reason to go to a church where there is fighting. Many have listened to the devil's advice, left me, and followed the wide road to destruction. Pray that your church will not fall into temptations like that. Ask my Father to deliver them from evil spirits and to help pull out all the destructive seeds of division in the church. You also need to understand that some spiritual leaders are not working for me, but for the devil. I didn't send them, but they pretend I called them to do my work. They don't rely on me, but rely on themselves. Those leaders promote themselves, not me. They use my name to gain other's approval and recognition. In fact, the devil loves these spiritually dead leaders because they help the devil to make more devil's children. But you have to rely on me so that you can handle the devil's attack with my power."

"Lord, what will happen to that lifeguard?"

"Suffering helps a person to have more compassion for others. The more suffering people experience, the more they are able to experience healing power through my words. When my workers recognize that my words can heal their wounds, they can use my medicine to heal other sick people. But I won't be pleased if my workers decide to listen to themselves and the world. The devil can plant seeds of bitterness, resentment, unforgiving attitude, and discouragement in their hearts. I will grieve if they turn their backs to me. My loving daughter, remember this; you will receive the reward when you run the race all the way and win. Not all of my workers receive a reward because many quit their race. You will grieve me if you quit the race because you couldn't handle criticism or rejection of others. Don't be discouraged when others misunderstand you. Not all of my children will understand that you are trying to walk with me because many don't understand other Christians' spiritual walk."

"Jesus, I need your forgiveness. For a long time, I didn't have much respect for the people who work for you. I thought they should work for the things they could see. I thought they were foolish to choose a difficult life and poverty. I didn't see much value in following you or working for your kingdom. Please forgive me."

"I forgive you, my daughter. When people

value what they can see, they may have a negative attitude toward my workers. You will meet many people like that when you work for me. I need to warn you about another thing as you do my work. I will show you what I mean."

As they walked along, they came to a big dark ship. A faint light coming from the stove burner was the only light. Blind and deaf people, who filled the ship, were sitting and drinking coffee. Some blind people fell into the river as they were walking. Some slipped and clung to the edge of the ship, exhausted, crying out for help; but no one came.

"Lord, Jesus, why is everyone on this ship blind and deaf? Why do they not have a lifeguard?"

"When people don't believe what I say about eternal hell, they are spiritually blind and spiritually deaf. My children receive rewards according to what they have done when they arrive at my Father's eternal home. Many people, even some of my workers, believe in a heavenly home, but do not believe that there is eternal burning hell for people who reject me. The devil is working hard to create distrust in my words, even in my children's hearts, so they don't look for the lost sheep. When people put their reasoning above my words, the devil paralyzes them to keep them from doing what I want them to do. Many of my children are sitting on a ship thinking they are safe when they don't even know which way to go. Anything contrary to my words, like human wisdom, does not have life but is like a destructive seed that originates from the flesh, the world, and the devil. If there were no eternal punishment and burning hell, why would I suffer and die to save people from their sin?"

The girl cried, "Jesus, please forgive me. I was spiritually blind and spiritually deaf. After you pulled me out of the river, I gave attention only to myself. I forgot that unbelievers would suffer eternally. I was safe, so I thought I didn't have to do anything to save other drowning people."

"Now do you understand why I called you to do my work? Do you understand why I am telling you that the harvest is plentiful but the workers are few?"

"Lord, I didn't realize how many are drowning in the river. How can I be a lifeguard? I don't even know how to swim."

"I will be teaching you how to swim. In order for you to be more fruitful, you also need to learn how to walk on water by faith. Then you will be able to save more people from drowning."

"How can I walk on the water?"

"In order to walk on the water and save people, you have to transform your mind and heart with my words. Humility is one of the requirements for being able to walk on the water and save people. You need to listen to the Holy Spirit. Otherwise, you will miss opportunities to rescue people. Nothing will be done by your power and wisdom. The Holy Spirit will direct you and give you discernment so that you will understand when, where, how, and to whom to reach out. Remember that you cannot use my power and wisdom to feed your pride. Otherwise you will fall after you lead others to God."

"Jesus, please help me to understand what it means to be humble before God."

"When people are not clothed with humility, they can not walk with me. Proud people cannot find me or see me because they are relying on themselves. When you lose sight of me and don't know which way to go, then remember, you have somehow fallen on account of pride. A proud attitude blinds a person's spiritual eyes. When that happens, repent, and find out how you lost the vision of me."

"Lord, for many years, I thought I had a strong faith and was spiritually mature; I fooled myself and fell with backsliding. That was when I didn't know where you were. How can I have a humble heart?"

Jesus said, "In order to walk humbly with me, you have to believe the power of my word and understand how the Holy Spirit works in you. You have to realize that my words are your life-giving spiritual food. Unless you keep reading my words to learn, you won't be able to learn how to be humble. My words have life-transforming power. Many of my workers believe their teaching can change other people's hearts, but without my powerful words and the Holy Spirit opening people's hearts to reveal their sins through my words, there will be no repenting, no salvation, no healing, and no transformation. Also, my words are a life-protecting sword to help people fight the enemy of the accusing voice, so they can be set free from all the burdens of guilt. My children are also called to use the sword to help others in bondage to set them free by telling them about the message of my love and forgiveness. Some use the sword to cut themselves to pieces by not forgiving themselves and others. Also, you have to recognize that all the glory belongs to God. When you start walking on the water and pulling out the drowning people, other people may recognize you as a lifeguard and start appreciating you. Don't give yourself credit, but realize that my powerful words and the Holy Spirit have done the mighty saving work. Give glory to God, be humble, and pray. Otherwise, you will fall into the sin of pride and be captured by the devil. Many of my workers fall into this trap. My power will not work in people who misuse it to promote themselves. I need humble workers who will use my words for my glory. Now you understand why my words have so much to do with humility."

"Yes, Lord, but my problem is that the more opportunity you provide for me to tell others about your love, and the more spiritual insights you give me, the more I have a chance to fall with pride. Even when I try to remind myself to be humble, that also becomes a hindrance; I compare myself with others and think I am more humble than others. So I am hopeless; I don't know how you can put up with me."

"When you focus on yourself and compare yourself to others, you will fall into a trap of boasting and having a proud attitude. Keep focusing your mind on me, not on yourself or others."

"Jesus, I still don't understand what humility is," the girl said.

"Humility is recognizing that the heavenly Father's way is better than yours. Humility is understanding God's will for your life and obeying it with a willing heart. Humility is obeying God even if it causes you pain and suffering. Humility is seeking God's kingdom first. Touch my hands, and learn from me."

The girl touched the holes in Jesus' hands and wept. "Lord, thank you for dying for my sins. Whenever I forget about the lesson of humility, please let me touch your hands." Jesus chose to show love even though it cost his life and his dignity. When people are motivated by love, they willingly take the road of suffering and humility for others. That's the love Jesus was asking of his disciples. That's the love Jesus was asking of her. If she loved Jesus, her sacrifice and difficulties wouldn't stop her from following Jesus. How others would see her was not important, she understood it.

"My beloved daughter, when you do my work, remember you are not alone. There are others who will be helping you by praying for you. Come, I will show you."

Jesus took her to a town with many churches. Some of them had thick white clouds in straight lines reaching up to heaven. Some had only a few lines of the clouds, and some didn't have any.

The girl looked at Jesus and asked, "Jesus, I have never seen anything like this. What are those lines of clouds?"

"My child, those are the heavenly phone lines of

my people who regularly communicate with my Father in heaven. Praying helps my children fight the spiritual battle and helps them clean out the garbage inside of themselves and others. My faithful servants pay attention to my words, follow the Holy Spirit's leading, and use those prayer lines consistently. I am standing with a basketful of heavenly spiritual blessings and am ready to pour them down. My people cannot imagine the things I have prepared for them. They will learn to hear my Father's voice when they start listening to the heavenly phone. The sad thing is that many of my children and my workers have forgotten to call my Father. They think they can handle their life and my work with their own wisdom and power, but nothing will be accomplished until people have my wisdom."

"My Lord, Jesus, I am sorry. I only prayed when I wanted something from you or when I was in trouble. I didn't realize that I need to pray to hear my Father's voice. I didn't pray to receive spiritual blessings, either."

"Many don't expect anything from me because they don't think I can do anything. People don't think I can give them power to reach out to many lost people. Pray so I will have many workers who can trust in my power to heal. I have much more to offer to my children. When people depend on me to release that power by praying, they will see miracles. You will be effective for my kingdom in proportion to how much you depend on my power by praying. I work with people who would depend on my power to change lives. Not only do you have to pray, to be effective you also have to be filled with the Holy Spirit. Follow me. I will show you what I mean."

Jesus took her to a town with many green houses. Each one had a gardener. Some gardeners had helpers with gardening books describing how to raise sweet plants in order to produce more sweet fruits. Some gardeners had more bitter plants, and they had ugly, strange looking animal creatures that brought more bitter plants to grow. Each gardener ate what he or she produced from their own garden and became either sick or healthy.

"My Lord, Jesus, what is happening here?"

"Each green house represents each person's heart. The plants represent what people are focusing on and to what they give energy and time. The helper is the Holy Spirit living inside a Christian's heart and helping with my gardening book of life which explains how to produce good fruits. The little animal creatures are the evil spirits who give people advice on how to grow bitter plants so people produce bitter fruits. The bitter plants produce the fruits of flesh, worldly, unspiritual, sinful desires and action. People with many bitter plants nurture pride, fear, jealousy, resentment, anger, hate, bitterness, selfishness, unforgiving hearts, and many other destructive attitudes and actions. The sweet trees produce the fruits of the Holy Spirit: humility, joy, godliness, forgiveness, love, hope, faith, unselfishness, faithfulness, perseverance, patience, compassion, thankful hearts, and many other positive attitudes and actions. Watch carefully your thoughts, attitudes, and motives, and see what you are planting because you will reap exactly what you sow. When you are planting bitter plants, you are piling up garbage in your heart. Garbage will burden you, and you won't be able to do what I am going to ask of you. In order to pull out the bitter plants and take the garbage out of your life, you need knowledge from the Scripture and the help of the Holy Spirit. You will be filled with the Holy Spirit as you plant sweet plants and produce sweet fruits in your heart. Unless your heart is filled with my words and with the Holy Spirit, you won't be able to do what I am going to ask you to do."

"Now I understand why you asked me to forgive people who hurt me. I didn't realize how much I was nurturing the seed of an unforgiving heart. Lord, help me to recognize which is a bitter seed and which is a sweet seed. Can you help so I will know what I am planting?"

Jesus said, "I have one thing to tell you, do you realize that my grace turned you around when you were heading toward the road of destruction?"

"I am sorry, Lord. I thought I was spiritually mature and was seeking you, so I was able to turn myself to you. But I couldn't have turned myself to you if you hadn't spoken to me and called me to do your work. I didn't even realize I was going the wrong way. I tried to give myself credit instead of recognizing your grace. I am learning that I cannot even trust my own judgments any more. Please forgive my ungrateful heart."

"I always forgive you my daughter," Jesus said, "I love you so much. I will give you anything, even my life, because I love you."

"I love you Jesus. You already have given your life for me, so I can be forgiven and live with you in our heavenly Father's home. Thank you so much."

Jesus replied, "But if I have to do it over again, I will die to save you because I love you, my child."

"Thank you Jesus. There is no one else like you. You care about me more than anyone else. Help me to hold on to your hand always."

"My daughter, you are worthy of my love. Come, follow me. I have something else to show you."

Jesus led her to a country church. Many people were arriving to attend the worship service. Some wore bright, shiny, white garments, and their faces were bright with big smiles. They were greeting and helping little children so they wouldn't fall.

Jesus' face beamed and he said proudly, "These are my workers. Many of them are not even recognized by others in the church, but I know who they are; they are the pillars of the church."

Some others who walked into the church wore dirty, filthy, and ragged garments. They each carried a plate in one hand as if they were ready to go through a cafeteria line. Some carried a sword in the other hand. Some started attacking others with their swords. Some were bleeding and had many cuts. Some carried heavy burdens on their back. Some carried ugly looking evil spirits on top of the burdens on their backs. Some arrived in wheelchairs with others' assistance. All of them carried pouches in front filled with sweet fruits and bitter fruits. Some shared their fruits with others.

Jesus turned to her and said, "My child, you need to understand that not all of the people who come to the church are saved. People who repented their sins and washed their sins with my blood wear white robes. People who haven't accepted my word and haven't repented their sins wear ragged garments."

"Lord, why are there so many wounded people here?" the girl asked.

"Many are going through the dark valley and along the roads of suffering. Pray so their wounds can be healed quickly, so they can help others who are suffering. My words are powerful medicine for the sick, they give encouragement to the discouraged, lift up the fallen, comfort the troubled, give hope to the hopeless, give help to the helpless, and revive the dying soul. These people come to my feast to feed their hungry souls."

"Why do some have swords and others don't have swords?"

"My words are like spiritual swords. However, many of my children are misusing them to be critical and judgmental of others and fall into the sin of pride. They don't understand that they have used the sword to fight the devil's accusing voices."

"Jesus, why do many still carry burdens on their backs. I thought Christians don't have to carry burdens because you have died on the Cross to free us."

"People who carry big burdens have not forgiven themselves or others. Many of my children suffer from the devil's accusing voice in their minds because they don't believe I forgive all of their sins. I call many of my children to serve me, but one of the reasons they don't respond is that they don't know how to forgive themselves and believe they are not worthy enough to work for me. I don't call people because they are worthy, but because they need me more than others do. Those I call to serve me are the ones that I give more spiritual hunger and thirst and the desire to know me. They can learn from me about my love and power and teach others about me. The devil knows whom I try to call to serve me, and he works hard to discourage them from following me. People have to understand that I come to call the sinners. I can use anyone who can accept my forgiveness and respond to my calling because my grace is sufficient for all. I don't even remember their sins anymore. I am still looking for people who can trust me completely and give their lives for revival."

"Lord, what about the devil on some people's backs? They are talking with the devil instead of listening to the Holy Spirit."

"Many are oppressed by the devil because they don't believe Satan exists. People don't have power to resist the devil unless they believe in me and use my name to resist it. Many of my children don't understand the spiritual battle, so the evil spirits hurt them and people think it is a natural cause. My words and the Holy Spirit will help the ones who diligently pray and trust my power. When my people put on the full armor of God, they will be able to win the spiritual battle."

"What about the pouches? What are they?"

"Everyone carries a fruit pouch with bitter or sweet fruits. The fruits are what they produce in their own garden in their hearts. The fruits each person brings to church will determine whether they will build up the body of Christ or be destructive to the body. Many are weak and need lots of care because they don't know how to nurture the sweet fruits in their hearts. People who believe in my power to heal will experience healing of the spirit and body. My child, do you understand why I am calling you to serve me?"

"Yes, my Lord, I feel overwhelmed by the work that needs to be done."

"Start with one person at a time. If you can find one lost sheep and help that person find me, then there will be joy in heaven. My Father will be pleased and there will be a feast because of that one person. Nothing you do for my kingdom is done by your wisdom or power. When you feel overwhelmed, you are not relying on me but yourself. When that happens, stop and pray to receive my wisdom. If you try to do my work with your own wisdom and power, you will fail. You need to pray to receive the power to spread the gospel to the ends of the world. Pray that God will give you heart to reach out to people who need salvation. Pray that God will open the doors so you will have more opportunity to reach out and bring many people to Christ. Pray that you will have revival in your heart. Unless you have revival in your heart, you won't be able to see the differences in other people's hearts when you minister to them. Others will experience revival in their hearts as much as you have experienced it. Follow me. I have another place to show you."

Jesus took her to a beautiful forest where colorful trees displayed their glory. It was so beautiful that she felt the glory with all her being. She couldn't believe that a place like that even existed. She ran around the trees, and when she got close to them, she was shocked to find out that the trees were not real but artificial.

She turned around and asked Jesus, "My Lord, these are not real. But if they are not real, how can I feel the beauty and glory in my soul?"

"There are many things in life that you will find so attractive and beautiful, and you can lose your heart to them. That is why many people love things in the world more than me. Sometimes what you love could be people, or people's wisdom, or man made things, or things I created. When you fill your heart with those, then you don't have any room for me. Whichever fills your heart will become your god. Anything that takes your heart away from me is what you should watch out for."

"Lord, what should I watch out for?"

"My daughter, do you realize that I gave you spiritual discernment so that you can help the body of

Christ. The reason I let you know who is walking with me or who is not walking with me is to help you know for whom you can pray. Instead, you are focusing on yourself and thinking how spiritually mature you are. You are misusing the gift I gave you. You are giving yourself glory. All the glory belongs to me, and when you focus on yourself with a boasting heart, you will lose sight of me."

"Please forgive me, Lord. I didn't even realize that."

"I forgive you. All the beauty in this world will pass away. The beauty you see in this world is only a shadow of heavenly glory. You have to realize that I am the one who gives beauty."

"Jesus, lately, I find beauty in other Christians because of their commitment to you and their knowledge about you."

"That's another thing you have to watch out for. You need to learn from other mature Christians, but your focus should be me. Make sure you don't put other's teaching above my words of life. You need to walk with me and learn from me, so you can learn to obey the Holy Spirit's instructions. Come, I have something else to show you."

After that, the girl visited the heavenly garden with Jesus where she felt God's love and beauty in her heart. Until then, she didn't know she could feel love in her heart. The beauty she felt there was something she had never experienced before. The sweet feeling she felt was so overwhelming that she wanted to stay in that garden forever. Reading the Scriptures, praising God by singing hymns, and spending time in prayer brought her more joy than anything.

As she walked along the path, suddenly, she was standing on a cliff all by herself. Jesus was already on the ground below stretching out his arms and asking her to come down. When she turned around to see the road she traveled, she was surprised to find it gone. She wanted to stay in the garden longer, but she couldn't.

Jesus called her, "My child, it's time for you to come down. I want you to feed others because that's why I have called you."

Reluctantly, she came down, and Jesus helped her to stand on her feet.

Jesus said, "My daughter, you can go back to the heavenly garden when you want, but you cannot stay there all the time. You cannot grow if you only feed yourself. You will grow more when you help others grow spiritually. Your testimony is also my testimony of how I have helped you. It is time for you to go out and tell others how I healed you. Ask me whatever you want, I will give it to you."

She thought for a moment, then said, "My Lord, Jesus, all those years I had my own visions, dreams, and hopes of what kind of person I wanted to be and what kind of life I wanted to live. I would like to understand your visions, dreams, and hopes for me. Also, you have been asking me to go out to help others, but I don't understand your love for them. I need to understand your love and power, so I can reach out to the people you want me to reach."

Jesus took her to the town that had the biggest hospital filled with wounded people. A little girl with one arm cut off, dripping blood, was crying out loud, trying to find her mother. People around her acted as though they didn't see her or hear her cry. There were only a few doctors and nurses busy helping too many people; no one was able to help her.

"My Lord, Jesus, why don't people help her?" The girl cried.

"My daughter, you are seeing only one of my daughters who is in pain. There are many who are suffering just like her. I need my workers to go out to heal the girl and others. Do you realize that you were like that girl, helpless and in need of an arm?"

"No, I didn't know that," the girl shook her head, tears streaming down her cheeks.

"Look closely at your right arm, the arm you always used to hold on to my hands."

The girl looked closely at her arm and found a scar on her skin. It was as though she had had surgery a long time ago. "What is this scar?" she questioned. "I have never seen this before."

"My daughter, the scar that you are seeing is your emotional scar. I have healed you. I have given you a new arm so you can hold my hand."

"Thank you, Lord. I didn't even realize that you have given me a new arm. Was the girl that I saw me?"

"Yes. I have carried you out of that place in my loving arms and healed you. You were so helpless, but I have power to heal. Now do you realize why others need to experience my healing power?"

The girl wept. She finally understood why Jesus had come to the world to save suffering people from sin. She also learned that she could not grasp other's suffering unless she experiences it or God grants her the opportunity to taste it without actually living through it. She was convinced that her decision to follow Jesus to help others was the right one.

"Jesus, how can I help these people? What do you want me to do?"

"Do you remember that I told you that we have work to do before we reach our heavenly Father's home?"

"Yes, Lord, what would you want me to do."

"My child, I am looking for people whom I can trust with my power to transform other people's lives. In order to have that power, you have to pay the price."

"What is the price I have to pay?" the girl asked, surprised.

Before Jesus answered, a man approached and showed the girl a turnip and explained how much it would cost. "It is $1,400," he said.

She thought if she could plant lots of turnips, she would make lots of money. Suddenly, she found herself standing in a large golden field ready for harvest. If she could plant turnips in that field, she could make lots of money, she said to herself. But there was no time to plow and plant because the field was ready for harvest.

Jesus said to her, "My daughter, do you

remember that I want you to reach out to the people in prison because I love them and I have died for them."

"Yes, Jesus."

"I am sending you to the prisons where the field is ready to harvest. You didn't plant. You didn't work hard to make it to that stage, but I am sending you so you can work as my worker. Go, I will go with you and show you wonders, and I will open people's hearts and save them. The price you have to pay is to go where I send you. Volunteer to give testimony in different prisons."

She understood then that God had answered her prayers asking for understanding of God's visions, dreams, and hopes for her. She didn't know how God would lead her, but one thing is sure: she could anticipate this harvest with the greatest anticipation she has ever had. God had never failed her or disappointed her. She knew she could bear lots of fruits according to God's wishes. However, that would be the case only if she would pay the price of going to prisons with a willing heart to tell the people about God's love and forgiveness.

Jesus said, "Remember we are on a journey to our heavenly Father's home. Before we arrive there, we have lots of work to do. Let's help others who need my love and healing. My beloved daughter, do you love me?"

"Yes, my Lord Jesus, I love you."

Jesus said, "If you love me, go out and find my lost sheep, and heal them with my words. I have died on the Cross for their sins, and my Father has forgiven them. Tell them they don't have to carry their burdens anymore because I have carried their burdens. Take care of them as I have been taking care of you. Take care of them as you would take care of me."

Jesus was so powerful. She had seen so many miracles because of Jesus. He not only healed her wounds and her backsliding, he also changed her heart and attitude toward the lost sheep.

She understood that she used to be one of the lost sheep. Jesus in his mercy pulled her out of the raging river. Until the Holy Spirit convicted her of her sins, she didn't even realize that she was a sinner. When God helped her to see her pitiful, hopeless, and sinful condition, she realized what was happening. She was carrying a heavy burden of sin, and the devil beat her down to the ground and tortured her by accusing her of the sins Jesus had paid for on the Cross. She cried and asked for God's forgiveness, and God forgave her.

The powerful words of God set her free from all condemnation. All her sins were nailed to the Cross when Jesus was nailed to the Cross. All of her sins died when Jesus died on the Cross. Her spirit came alive with the pure, spotless garment of holiness when Jesus rose from the dead. God had forgiven her, and no one could condemn her, not even herself. Jesus' blood washed all of her sins white as snow. She had experienced it.

She understood that whoever believes in Jesus

will experience this forgiveness and freedom because God won't remember their sins any more. There is no condemnation for those who are in Christ because of his sacrificial death on the Cross. Because Jesus showed her his love and care when she desperately needed to be free from the burden of sin, she understood how important it is to reach out to the lost sheep. It would be a terrible sin if she didn't share this wonderful message of forgiveness with others who are suffering from the burden of guilt.

Not all the roads she had walked with Jesus were easy. It was hard for her to understand why Jesus told her that the road of suffering was the road that she had to follow. While she was in tears walking through the thorn bushes with Jesus, she couldn't understand why Jesus wouldn't lead her to an easy path.

However, she understood that Jesus didn't create her misery and suffering. As Jesus told her, she was living in a fallen world where people are spiritually sick and sinful, influenced by fallen angels and the devil. Those things produce suffering. Jesus had love and compassion for suffering people. Jesus knew what people needed. He suffered so others wouldn't suffer.

Jesus provided forgiveness, eternal salvation, and healing, so people could live with perfect joy, peace, comfort, and freedom in the midst of difficulties and suffering while in the imperfect world. It was painful for her to follow the roads of suffering, but the tears and suffering helped her to experience

Jesus' healing power, love, and compassion. Through her suffering, Jesus gave her insights on how others are suffering and need healing.

Some roads she had walked were shameful because she didn't take Jesus' words seriously. Instead of listening to Jesus, she listened to herself and the world. She took the road of deception. She loved the world more than Jesus. Still Jesus forgave her, and cared for her all the way, even when she was not faithful to him. She was snatched out of the fire. Jesus was the one who pulled her out of a pit and saved her many times. Jesus' blood washed all of her shame from the past, present, and future. Jesus' blood has power to wash not only her sins, but those of all who come to Jesus and believe in him.

She learned that in order to follow Jesus, she not only had to let go of worldly desires and things that she enjoyed before, but she had to change her attitudes and her lifestyle. She had to change her priorities. Going back to the narrow road was painful because following Jesus required a denial of her easy way of life. She understood what her cross was, and instead of ignoring that cross, she made a commitment to carry it and follow Jesus.

It was a tearful, long process to follow Jesus, and not many understood why she had to follow Jesus the way she was. That brought tears because she had to go against people who were very dear to her. She had to make choices. She had to evaluate her motivation and reasons for following Jesus. She made up her mind to follow Jesus, not others. That caused tensions.

Obviously, she needed that purifying fire to find out how far she was willing to follow Jesus. That fire helped her to see herself better even though it was painful. Even in the midst of going through the purifying fire, she had experienced Jesus' love which helped her understand that God's grace is sufficient in all circumstances.

What Jesus said was true. She didn't belong to this world, but to Jesus. He called her out of the world. For a long time she thought the world was her permanent place to live, but then she learned that was her misconception. As she walked with Jesus, she learned how to say goodbye to every town she passed. As Jesus lead her, he had lessons to teach her in different towns, mountains, and deep dark valleys, so she could be a better servant for God's kingdom. Understanding Jesus became her highest priority, so she started reading the Scriptures more, especially the gospels.

Whenever she thought about how much Jesus loved her and how he even gave his life to save her, her heart was filled with joy and gratitude. Jesus loved her more than anyone else she had met on the road.

Jesus is so loving and powerful. She has seen only a glimpse of Jesus' glory, but someday, he will lead her to her heavenly Father's eternal home where there is no suffering, no tears, no mourning, no worry, no pain, no sickness, no terror, no despair, no death, no trials, no discouragement, no fears, no disappointment, no backsliding, no heartaches, no temptation, and no deception.

Instead of meeting Jesus in her heart, she will be able to see Jesus' loving face and touch him and tell him how much she loves him. She has been thinking about what she wants to do when she sees Jesus face to face. She will fall down to worship him and hold on to Jesus' right leg and thank him for walking with her and saving her from all the dangers while she was living on earth. Until then, she knows what she has to do. Her duty is to tell others how much Jesus loved her and forgave her, so others can understand how much Jesus loves them and forgives their sins.

She learned that there are too many lost sheep in the world. Jesus is the only one who can save people and give them hope.

The girl understands what will happen when she obeys the Holy Spirit:

Jesus will go out with her to search for the lost sheep.
Jesus will be carrying the lost sheep in his arms.
Jesus will heal and take care of the wounded sheep.
Jesus will help her to take care of the lost sheep with God's love and power.
Jesus will always walk with her and tell her that he loves her.
Jesus will lead her to the heavenly Father's home safely.
Jesus will welcome her when she arrives at the heavenly Father's home.

Part Three:
A Love Letter From Jesus

As I was preparing for my "Forgiveness" class at Denver Women's Correctional Facility, my friend gave me an idea about how people can experience Jesus' love by writing a letter from Jesus. I wrote this letter for my forgiveness class. I tried to imagine how Jesus would write to me. You can also write a letter from Jesus. Be creative and reflective. In the process, God may be speaking to you and you may hear God's voice.

My precious child, I watched you walking alone on the street. You looked so lonely, as if no one would understand how sad you were. I saw your gentle face with tears streaming down your cheeks, as if no one cared about you. The wind dried your tears. My pierced hands also dried your tears. Come to me and talk to me when you are sad and lonely. I will always listen and give you comfort. Remember, I care about you more than you can imagine or think. I created you and gave you life. You are my child. I can share my deepest love with everyone who comes to me. Come to me. I am Jesus, your friend. You deserve my love.

My wonderful child, I saw you lying in bed. The moonlight was the only light in your room. When no one else was looking, I saw your tears of grief and sorrow. You didn't think anyone could understand you. I wanted you to turn to me so you could be comforted. You did turn to me as you went to sleep. I wiped your tears, and you didn't even realize it. The pillow you had was my soft arm. You went to sleep in my arms. I understand you. There is no one who can give you peace and comfort as I can. Come to me. I am Jesus, your friend. You deserve my love.

My beloved child, I heard you asking for forgiveness. I checked your record, and I couldn't find the sins you were mentioning. In case you were talking about your old sins, the ones that you have already repented and thus erased from my record, I need to remind you that I cannot remember your sins any more. I never condemn you for anything. My gift for you is my life. On the cross, I endured anguish, torture, and pain and suffering so that you could be forgiven. I poured out my blood to forgive you and pardon you. I paid the price for your sins with my life. I clothe you with beautiful, spotless, and holy garments. You are so lovely, and there is no way I can forget about you, not even for a moment. You are forgiven, my child. I want to see your smiling face, knowing that you are free, because I have forgiven your sins of the past, present, and future. You are innocent. I can forgive everyone who comes to me. Come to me. I am Jesus, your friend. You deserve my love.

My gentle child, I saw you standing before the mirror reflecting on your past. I saw your tears of regret, remorse, shame, and guilt. You were sad that you couldn't share what happened to you with others.

I saw your heart bleeding from the wounds. My heart ached with sorrow. Why? You didn't commit any sins when you were not in control of situations that involved other people's words and behaviors. I am sorry about what happened to you. The Holy Spirit has the power to heal your wounds and painful memories. My child, I feel the pain of your suffering. I have compassion for everyone who comes to me. Come to me. I am Jesus, your friend. You deserve my love.

My beautiful child, I saw you carrying burdens of guilt and shame on your back. When you collapsed on the ground, the devils tried to put more burdens on your back by accusing you of past sins and reminding you of others' hurtful words and behaviors. I saw your tears of helplessness and hopelessness. Why? It was because you thought I have not forgiven your sins. You thought I have no power to help you. That brought tears to my eyes. I have suffered for you and carried your burdens, so you don't have to carry those burdens any more. I want you to look at me and see my tears. I want you to touch my pierced hands and receive my forgiveness. Give all your burdens to me so I can heal your wounds. You can have my peace and joy. Remember everyone makes mistakes. It is time to forgive yourself and others because I have forgiven you. I died on the Cross to free you from all your burdens. Hold my hands, and get up and walk with me. Look up to me, and listen to my voice; then you will see my face. Listen to my words, and understand what I have done for you.

Your sins were nailed to the Cross. My blood has power to free everyone who comes to me. You are free and forgiven. Come to me. I am Jesus, your friend. You deserve my love.

My delightful child, I danced with you in my garden today. Your prayer brought joy to me. I was delighted that you remembered me and came to me. Your gentle voice touched my heart so much that I wanted to dance more with you. It was your smile that brought a smile to my face. If you can dance with me by listening to me and talking to me, you will be able to handle the difficult situations with my power, the Holy Spirit. I want you to understand how much I love you. How sweet you are to me. You are like the light that shines in the early, fresh garden where the roses bloom. You are like the bright, shining star that decorates my glorious sky. I can share my deepest thoughts with everyone who comes to me. Come to me. I am Jesus, your friend. You deserve my love.

My glorious child, I love you more than my life. You are my joy and my glory. Receive my love. Your love is all I ask. I invite you to my table, that glorious, heavenly banquet that my Father has prepared for my children. I want you to see that your cup overflows because of the Holy Spirit's healing presence. I want you to walk with me so you can hear my voice and see my shining face filled with love for you. The Holy Spirit can fill you with visions, dreams, hopes, joy, peace, love, and power. I can give my gift of the Holy Spirit to everyone who comes to me. Receive spiritual blessings that I have prepared for you. Receive the

Holy Spirit. Come to me. I am Jesus, your friend. You deserve my love.

My powerful child, I have called you to minister to proclaim the message of forgiveness to those who are hurting, so others can experience the healing power of the Holy Spirit. Rely on the Holy Spirit's power to heal and transform you, and then others can experience what you have experienced through your ministry. Most of all, you always have to remember that all the glory belongs to me, no one else. I am looking for people whom I can trust with the power to heal and transform others. If you can die to worldly desires, have my compassion, and obey the Holy Spirit, then you can experience healing and transforming power in yourself and in others. Come and follow me. I am Jesus, your friend. You deserve my love.

My beloved child, It is time to go out and reach out to those who are suffering. Can you hear their cry? Can you feel their pain? Can you see their wounds? Can you understand what the Holy Spirit can do to help them? Many are living in emotional turmoil because they don't know me. Many innocent people are walking the roads of suffering because of injustices done to them. Many carry heavy burdens of guilt because they don't understand what I have done for them. Many are tormented by the devil's accusing voices because they don't know how to resist the devil by the power of the Holy Spirit. Many are lonely and sad and they need to be reminded of my love and power. Many do not have visions and dreams because they don't understand the plans that I have for them. Many feel helpless to help others because they don't understand the healing and transforming power of the Holy Spirit. Rely on my powerful words, pray constantly, and follow the Holy Spirit's guidance, so you will be filled with the Holy Spirit. Then others can experience healing and transformation through you. The Holy Spirit has unlimited power to transform and heal those who are suffering, and I want you to experience that power because I live in you and you live in me. Come to my feast. I am Jesus, your friend. You deserve my love.

Part Four: A Prayer of Blessing

I pray that you will be blessed
and experience Jesus every moment.
So that you will hear His voice clearly,
see His compassionate face,
feel His gentle arms carrying you,
understand His urgent calling,
follow Him immediately to serve Him,
love Him with all your being,
give Him all you have,
obey Him till death,
see His glory,
and experience healing.

Part Five:
The Healing Power of Jesus

To those who are searching for the meaning of life, and to those who want to experience healing, I ask you to invite Jesus not only into your heart but into every area of your life. When you have Jesus in every area of your life, you will be transformed.

Inviting Jesus into your life does not mean that all your problems will be solved. As long as we live in this world, there will be problems. Life is full of natural disasters, and sickness comes because our physical bodies have limitations We all die eventually, and no one is exempt from it. In many cases, life is not fair. Many suffer because people make bad decisions, are selfish, and are not sensitive to others' pain.

Life is already hard because of our own limitations and others' mistreatment of us. But some suffer more because they seem to believe God is the cause of suffering or God mistreated them by allowing bad things to happen to people. They believe God is a mean and cruel God who loves to see people in pain. Moreover, people who believe this way have a difficult time believing that God loves them. When bad things happen, some believe that God is punishing them. This concept of God, I believe, has plagued many people, and this belief is against Jesus' teaching. Instead of meeting a comforting, caring, forgiving and healing God, some reject God because they misunderstand God's loving nature.

I do not believe God is the one who causes

suffering. Natural disasters can happen to any one of us, but that does not prove God is the cause of suffering. I have met people who believe God caused suffering when in reality other people have hurt them. Some even blame God for their own mistakes.

We need to take responsibility for our own attitudes and actions and not blame God. God does not hurt us through other people. We all make mistakes and that is why we need God's forgiveness. God knows we make mistakes. He knows how we feel and what we are going through.

God has more love for us than we can imagine. God's desire for us is to experience healing through Jesus. Even though other people may not understand us, Jesus understands our hearts and knows what we are going through. Jesus feels our pain and suffering and that is why He came to save us and died on the cross for our sins. He showed His love through His actions. Jesus is for us, not against us. He understands our hearts more than anyone. Inviting Jesus in is also to recognize our weaknesses and mistakes and to accept God's forgiveness and to learn to forgive ourselves and others who have hurt us.

Not only does Jesus love us, but He also has power to help us. He can help us in times of trouble by giving us comfort and peace. He also gives us wisdom and courage to work things out when we rely on Him to solve problems. Jesus has so much to offer, and when you believe in Jesus, you receive the gift of the Holy Spirit who can teach and direct us. The Holy Spirit can teach us about Jesus through the Bible and gives us gifts which enable us to help others who are suffering.

Many of us are going through suffering, some more

than others. We are living in a world surrounded with people who are suffering. When I was working as an intern Chaplain at Denver Women's Correctional Facility, I attended a graduation ceremony for the Therapeutic Community one afternoon in the spring of 2000. During the ceremony, an inmate gave a speech about what Therapeutic Community was about. The whole time she was giving the presentation, tears streamed down her cheeks and many of us also wept along with her. That experience taught me how much people are in pain and suffering and are in need of Christ.

I also experienced the power of Jesus. One day as I was in a housing unit, an inmate who looked disturbed approached me. She told me that she was having a difficult time because she was hearing voices behind her and seeing things that others did not see. She had a long history of mental problems. I learned that she believed in God and Jesus. She was not attending worship services at the time. As I was listening to her, I thought what she needed was spiritual healing.

I didn't have any doubt that if she believed in Jesus and proclaimed Jesus' power to resist the devil, she would be freed from her problems.

The woman was not convinced of the spiritual influences. I told her that what happened in Bible times can happen to her, and she can experience healing. This is possible through the power of Jesus and by saying, "In the name of Jesus, you devil, leave me." Still, she was not convinced.

About three months later, she stopped me in the housing unit again. This time she was radiant. She had to tell me what happened. Since I had talked to her the last time, an inmate asked her to attend a worship service.

She went with her. There, people believed the same way I did about her illness. She followed their suggestion. She proclaimed Jesus' power and told the devil to leave. Once she did that, she no longer had problems with voices or seeing things. Since then she has started attending worship services regularly and prays to Jesus everyday.

She became a firm believer that Jesus has the power to heal people. She learned to rely on Jesus to resist the spiritual influences and not on other people. Unless the person believes in Jesus' power, it is difficult to restore the person's spiritual health. She told me that her doctor was surprised to find out that she was healed.

I do not believe all mental illness can be cured in this way. Some people have brain damage, and some need medical care. In fact, in many cases, doctors can help restore health. They are doing God's work that way, but in some cases, people need spiritual healing, and this was such a case.

This event gave me more confidence in God who has more love and power to heal us. People can experience healing through accepting the love and power of Jesus. Jesus can heal our painful memories and help us to forgive. Jesus can do so much through us if we are willing to follow Him and have the commitment to do what He is asking us to do. Jesus has the transforming power to change us and others. That is why I am asking you to invite Jesus, not only into your hearts, but into every area of your life.

Part Six: Invitation

1. AN INVITATION TO ACCEPT CHRIST – Words of invitation from the F Module Pod 1300 & Prayer written by D Module Pod, 5 Maximum Saints from the Adams County Detention Facility.

Are you questioning God? Do you lift your hands in frustration and cry? Have you created an unbearable amount of pain in your life, that you cannot handle! Are loved ones on the outside reaching out to you, but they can no longer touch you? Is there an incredible emptiness and pain in your stomach that no one understands? A pain that no one can take away? No more questioning, but now is the time to act. Don't delay.

Bow down. Let the One who created the world lift your burdens, and cleanse your soul. Let Jesus' love, hope, joy fill you to the maximum. Jesus can help you deal with pain when no one can. He can give you peace when no one can. Here is a prayer that you can pray if you would like to invite Christ into your heart so you can be saved and experience the peace of Christ in your heart.

Prayer: "Dear Jesus, I am prepared to invite you into my heart, mind, body, and soul. I come before you offering myself as a living sacrifice, confessing my sins and weaknesses. Father, I put all my trust in you, and I want You to have total control over my life. I am sorry, Lord, for the things I have done that grieve you and others. Please forgive me for all my sins. I ask that the distractions around me be put on hold, so that I will be able to receive you into my life today. Please send your

Holy Spirit into my heart and give me the power to live a new life in Christ. Thank you Lord for your love, and I give my life to you in the name of Jesus. Amen"

"That if you confess with your mouth, 'Jesus is Lord,' and believe in your heart that God raised him from the dead, you will be saved." (Romans 10:9) "If we confess our sins, he is faithful and just and will forgive us our sins and purify us from all unrighteousness." (1 John 1:9) "Salvation is found in no one else, for there is no other name under heaven given to men by which we must be saved." (Acts 4:12) "In him we have redemption through his blood, the forgiveness of sins" (Eph.1:9).

2. AN INVITATION TO DONATE BOOKS FOR THE JAIL AND PRISON MINISTRY

With 1,300 some inmates we are always short of Christian books. Many inmates have requested books written by Mary Baxter, especially "A Divine Revelation of Hell," and I have witnessed encouraging transformations in inmates who have read her books. I figured it would take 600 copies of Mary Baxter's books for our facility - 400 copies in English and 200 in Spanish – but to purchase that many books we would need $6,000. Then one day an idea came to me. If I were to find 100 churches or 100 individuals who would donate one book a month, just $10 a month, that would be one more book the inmates would have to read. That's when, with the help of many good friends and inmate leaders, I started the Transformation Project in 2005. More than ten churches are participating in this project at the present time, and I will keep promoting this ministry opportunity in different churches until our goal is reached. More churches began to participate in the ministry in our facility because of the Transformation Project. YOU could be involved with this project also by donating a book a month by sending just $10 monthly to the Transformation Project. Also, when you donate $10 for each copy of the "Maximum Saints Production" book, we can distribute 9 books for free in jails and prisons. (If you have any questions about how you can start the Transformation Project in your church, and participate in this "Maximum Saints Productions" book donation project, please call the Chaplains at 303-655-3311.)

<u>Donations may be sent to:</u>

Park Hill United Methodist Church
Transformation Project:
Prison Ministry
5209 Montview Boulevard
Denver, CO, 80207
(Chaplains do not handle the funds.)

The chaplain's office is always looking for good religious books. Second-hand books, in good condition, can be donated to the chaplain's office. However, we prefer the books that the inmates request as much as possible. Any books written by Mary Baxter, the "Left Behind" series by Tim LaHaye and Jerry B. Jenkins, "The Purpose Driven Life" by Rick Warren, and any books by Charles Stanley that might be sitting on your book shelf may be donated to our facility. Please mail them to:

Adams County Detention Facility
Chaplain's Office
150 North 19th Ave.

Brighton, CO 80601.

3. AN INVITATION TO COMMENT

If this book has touched you and you want to share that, please send us your comments. Your letters may be sent to:

Fort Lupton First United Methodist Church
Maximum Saints Productions:
Prison Ministry
306 Park Ave.
Fort Lupton, CO 80621-1930
Phone: (303) 857-2257

3. AN INVITATION TO PARTICIPATE IN FUTURE "MAXIMUM SAINTS" BOOKS

(1) If you are incarcerated at the Adams County Detention Facility, please submit your story to your facility chaplain for the future publication of the book, "Maximum Saints."
(2) For all others who are incarcerated in other facilities, and would like to submit your stories of how Jesus has helped you for the future "Maximum Saints" book, you can send your stories to Fort Lupton First United Methodist Church Maximum Saints Productions: Prison Ministry (address above).
(3) For those who in the past have been incarcerated and have experienced transformation because of God's love, and are now released and involved in some kind of ministry, please send your stories to: Maximum Saints Productions (address on pg 125).
(4) We invite those who have received life sentences

or death sentences to share how God has helped you to handle your painful journeys, changing them into journeys of hope and peace. We especially would like you to share about how you have helped others with the issues of depression, forgiveness, and grieving— from losses and how to let them go, and from the death of a loved one. If you have dealt with people around you who are facing death, or if you are facing death, a terminal illness or execution, please send your stories to Maximum Saints Productions (address on pg 125). Please write what helped you the most when you were going through painful times and what changed your perception and your life. Your stories of how your life changed from one of despair to one of hope will help many others who are going through tough times.

Please send us your story for possible publication which may be in the form of: testimonies, sermons, poems, songs, prayers, or drawings. In addition, you can submit the love letters or forgiveness letters you have written to your family or to others. Because others might not want you to use their names, we might change the name of your wife or husband, or other family member or friends. Send to: Maximum Saints Productions (address on pg 125).

Please enclose the following permission letter:

"I, <u>your name</u>, give permission to the Maximum Saints Productions to print my story. My name may/may not be used. I understand that I will not receive any royalties from the sale of these books. I also understand that my manuscript might be edited for the book.

Your signature and date."
(Your manuscript will not be returned to you; therefore, please keep a copy of what you send.)

Without a permission letter containing the information requested in the example letter above, the Maximum Saints Productions will not publish any stories that are submitted. If you mail your story, and the church selects it, your story will be published in the book, *Maximum Saints Can Move Mountains.* Thank you for your participation.

Maximum Saints Productions is looking for stories of how others have been transformed to help and encourage both the incarcerated and their families, to bring healing through the love and power of Christ.

Please <u>do not</u> send any letter or story to the Chaplains of the Adams County Detention Facility since the facility does not allow inmates to correspond with chaplains.

Anyone who would like to send a donation for this book project to help with spreading them to other jails and prisons, please send your check to:

Park Hill United Methodist Church
Transformation Project: Prison Ministry.
5209 Montview Boulevard
Denver, CO, 80207
Phone: (303) 322-1867

Invitation

4. TO PURCHASE BOOKS

Journey With Jesus, Maximum Saints Never Hide in the Dark, and other books by Yong Hui V. McDonald may be purchased through our website: www.firstlovepress.com, or call 720-427-5323. The books may also be purchased at the Bible Discount Book Store, 6896 Highway 2, Commerce City, CO 80022 - Phone: 303-287-7777. The cost of any of the above books is $10 plus shipping and handling. To send a book to someone who is incarcerated contact either First Love Press or Bible Discount Book Store and, if the facility allows inmates to receive books from book stores, the book/books will be sent directly to the inmate.

"I was honored to be in attendance during chaplain's worship when a lot of these testimonies and sermons were being delivered, and to see the tears and the pure, raw sincerity in the eyes of these inmates as they spilled their hearts to God and strangers alike was an unforgettable inspiration."
— Michael O'Connor, Chaplains' Assistant, an inmate at the Adams County Detention Facility, Brighton, Colorado

Part Seven: Beauty of Jesus

In my fall quarter of 2001 I was driving home and listening to a hymn, "Lord, you are more precious than silver. Lord, you are more costly than gold. Lord, you are more beautiful than diamonds." I prayed to God to help me experience the beauty of Jesus. Three days later, I was heading back to Denver to go to school. As soon as I started driving on the highway, I saw a big image of Jesus wearing a royal robe, and his heart was bleeding all the way down. There was more blood on the bottom part of the robe. It seemed His heart may have been bleeding for quite some time.

I was distressed at what I saw. That image lingered before me for awhile and even though there were no words, I understood that someone had pierced His heart with a spear. That reminded me of a Bible story. After Jesus had died on the cross, a soldier pierced Jesus' side. *"But when they came to Jesus and found that he was already dead, they did not break his legs. Instead, one of the soldiers pierced Jesus' side with a spear, bringing a sudden flow of blood and water."* (John 19:33-34) What I saw was only the thick blood. Then, a thought came to me, "You said you wanted to understand Jesus' beauty."

I still could not understand why I saw the distressing image of Jesus. I asked to see Jesus' beauty, not an image of Jesus' suffering. Again, an understanding came to me. "Jesus' beauty is to feel others' pain. When people have pain, Jesus feels that pain." I broke down in tears at the thought of Jesus' great love and his suffering for humanity. I was convinced again that helping others who are suffering also eases Jesus' pain. I learned that inner beauty is to understand others' pain and to empathize and do something about it. I was comforted by the fact that Jesus feels my pain and my suffering and I am grateful that I am called to help and comfort those who are suffering.

God taught me many things through my prison ministry.

God taught me about suffering of incarcerated people and how some inmate leaders are helping others to ease that pain. When I was working as an intern chaplain at the Denver Women's Correctional Facility, I attended a Therapeutic Community (T.C.) graduation ceremony. One inmate completed all the courses and all of her classmates and many volunteers were there to celebrate her accomplishment. In that ceremony, one of the classmates was giving a presentation on the purpose of the class. When she started reading her manuscript, she had a difficult time reading it because she was choked with emotion, and she couldn't stop her tears. The whole presentation lasted about five minutes, but I felt it was eternity because she was weeping the whole time. Many who attended the ceremony wept, and I couldn't stop my tears. For the first time in my life, I felt the suffering of humanity with my whole being through this woman.

After I started working at the Adams County Detention Facility, I also came in contact with many who experienced so much pain and suffering. One day, I saw so many song sheets that we used for Chaplain's Worship services that had water spots. There were so many that I had a hard time reading the words. I asked an inmate chaplain's assistant what caused the water spots on the song sheets. I asked him if the water spots came from baptisms since we had so many baptisms. He said, "No. Many people were weeping in worship services and that's why many song sheets had spots. I had to wipe the tears from the song sheets." Then I realized how many inmates were going through tough times. At the same time, I believed God was bringing healing through these tears. Tears are prayers of our hearts. God listens to our prayers of tears. Tears also show the deep pain in our hearts. As long as we can cry and weep before the Lord, and our hearts are broken, there is hope for healing through the Holy Spirit.

Another discovery is that many inmate leaders recognize other's pain and they are doing something to help others to ease that pain. I believe no one can minister to other inmates better than inmates, since they are with others for 24 hours. I have met many powerful inmate leaders who found Christ, and they share Christ's love with others because they know Jesus can help others.

For a long time, I wanted to see a revival in America and I have experienced it at the Adams County Detention Facility. I have

*"Jesus' beauty is to feel others' pain.
When people have pain, Jesus feels that pain."*

Beauty of Jesus 131

seen the glimpse of God's glory and the Holy Spirit's power through these leaders. I am proud to announce to the world that many of our facility inmate leaders, whom I call "Maximum Saints," are making a difference in the lives of many other inmates. Many inmate leaders are leading Bible study and prayer meetings in their own pods to help others. These leaders serve the Lord in the midst of going through the fires of testing. They know how to help others who are desperate in need of comfort and encouragement. These inmates are fearless for the Lord. They bring hope, healing and inspiration in a place where distrust and violence can bring more suffering to many.

To help ease the pain of others, if you feel God is calling you to serve Him, don't waste your time any more. Make plans to serve Him completely by preparing to go into the ministry and to obey what God has called you to do. Jesus said, *"The harvest is plentiful, but the workers are few. Ask the Lord of the harvest, therefore, to send out workers into his harvest field." (Luke 10:2-3)*

Give your life to Christ and serve Him, not just with words but with actions. I assure you, you will not regret it. If you give 100% to God, you will receive much more in return. Serve God even when you are incarcerated to bring hope and healing to others who are suffering. Those who are longing to see a revival, don't just pray, but act on your faith and ask the Holy Spirit to guide you to serve the Lord to the maximum. If you go beyond your own pain but look into other's pain and help them, you will experience healing. I encourage you to serve Christ whether you are incarcerated or not. You will be much happier if you obey the Lord. God bless you!

"For God so loved the world that He gave His one and only Son, that whoever believes in Him shall not perish but have eternal life." (John 3:16) "The Spirit of the Lord is on me, because he has anointed me to preach good news to the poor. He has sent me to proclaim freedom for the prisoners and recovery of sight for the blind, to release the oppressed, to proclaim the year of the Lord's favor." (Luke 4: 18-19) "Come to me, all you who are weary and burdened, and I will give you rest. Take my yoke upon you and learn from me, for I am gentle and humble in heart, and you will find rest for your souls. For my yoke is easy and my burden is light." (Matthew 11:28-30)